PENGU

INTE

Noam Chomsky has been described as the world's greatest public intellectual. He is the author of numerous bestselling political books, including *Hegemony or Survival*, *Imperial Ambitions*, *Failed States*, *Perilous Power* and *What We Say Goes*. He is also a professor in the Department of Linguistics and Philosophy at MIT, and is widely credited with having revolutionized modern linguistics. He lives in Lexington, Massachusetts.

Peter Hart is the activism director at FAIR, the national media watchdog group.

Interventions
Noam Chomsky

PENGUIN BOOKS

PENGUIN BOOKS

Published by the Penguin Group
Penguin Books Ltd, 80 Strand, London WC2R 0RL, England
Penguin Group (USA), Inc., 375 Hudson Street, New York, New York 10014, USA
Penguin Group (Canada), 90 Eglinton Avenue East, Suite 700, Toronto, Ontario, Canada M4P 2Y3
(a division of Pearson Penguin Canada Inc.)
Penguin Ireland, 25 St Stephen's Green, Dublin 2, Ireland (a division of Penguin Books Ltd)
Penguin Group (Australia), 250 Camberwell Road, Camberwell, Victoria 3124, Australia
(a division of Pearson Australia Group Pty Ltd)
Penguin Books India Pvt Ltd, 11 Community Centre, Panchsheel Park, New Delhi – 110 017, India
Penguin Group (NZ), 6
(a division of Pearson
Penguin Books (South

Penguin Books Ltd, Re

www.penguin.com

First published in the
First published in Grea
Published in Penguin
3

Copyright © Noam Ch
All rights reserved

The writings in this bc
distributed by the New

The moral right of the

Printed in Great Britain by Clays Ltd, St Ives plc

ISBN: 978-0-141-03180-4

www.greenpenguin.co.uk

Mixed Sources
Product group from well-managed
forests and other controlled sources
www.fsc.org Cert no. SA-COC-1592
© 1996 Forest Stewardship Council
FSC

Penguin Books is committed to a sustainable future
for our business, our readers and our planet.
The book in your hands is made from paper
certified by the Forest Stewardship Council.

Table of Contents

Editor's Note
by Greg Ruggiero

For the past seventeen years Noam Chomsky has contributed many titles to the Open Media Series, including his runaway international bestseller, *9-11*, and the work that launched the series itself—a transcript of an antiwar speech Chomsky gave at Harvard University in November 1990. What few people have known, me included until very recently, is that in the months after his *9-11* hit the *New York Times* extended bestseller list, Chomsky began producing concise essays, approximately 1,000 words each, distributed by The New York Times Syndicate as op-eds.

Chomsky's op-eds have been picked up widely by the international press, but much less so in the United States where "newspapers of record" have declined to publish them. None of the essays distributed by the Syndicate have appeared in the *New York Times*, *Los Angeles Times*, *Washington Post* or *Boston Globe*, though they have been picked up and published by a few regional papers, like the *Register Guard*, the *Dayton Daily News*, and the *Knoxville Voice,* a Tennessee-based monthly.

That our mainstream media system seems unwilling to tolerate a range of political thought wide enough to include Chomsky's but *is* willing to market them outside our intellectual and geographic borders is ironic and revealing. Tariq Ali says that "if Chomsky were living in Italy, Germany, France, or Britain, he would have a regular column in one of those coun-

tries' major newspapers." Chomsky's columns have appeared
in the mainstream British press, including the *International
Herald Tribune*, the *Guardian*, and the *Independent*. One of
Mexico's national newspapers, *La Jornada*, publishes Chomsky
frequently; it just hasn't happened yet in Chomsky's home
country.

It is thus a great honor to present readers in the United
States with *Interventions*, a complete collection of the op-eds
Chomsky has written to date for The New York Times Syndicate, minus one or two that were verbatim excerpts from his
recent books. *Interventions* also includes one piece—"A Wall As
a Weapon"—written specifically for the *New York Times*, not
for the Syndicate, two parts of the same company. Chomsky
has taken the occasion of producing this collection to add notes
and, in some cases restore passages from his original drafts that
had been edited out for reasons of space. He also added material expanding what was in the original drafts—background,
and other information. As a book, *Interventions* has benefited
from these additions.

It is important to note that during the period that Chomsky
wrote the essays in this book—2002 to 2007—he also wrote
several major works: *Hegemony or Survival* (which held ground
for weeks on the *New York Times* bestseller list after Hugo
Chávez praised it during a speech before the United Nations in
2006), *Failed States* and *Perilous Power* (with Gilbert Achcar
and Stephen Shalom), all of which discuss many of the ideas
contained in *Interventions* in greater detail.

In composing op-eds, Chomsky is taking advantage of the
fact that our society is still one of the freest in the world: open-
ings still exist to challenge the White House, the Pentagon, and
the corporations enriched by them. Chomsky believes that the
freedom to challenge power is not just an opportunity, it's

a responsibility, and he takes advantage of the op-ed form to do just that. These brief, fiercely–argued essays were written in order to reach readers in the popular, shared space of their daily newspapers, and Chomsky demonstrates that he can just as persuasively strike at the heart of today's political contradictions, deceptions, and hidden horrors with a few hundred words as he can with a few hundred pages.

Despite the profound inequities in this country and the nightmare of being a nation at war, Chomsky reminds us that ordinary people still have power to drive change. "One of the clearest lessons of history," he writes, "including recent history, is that rights are not granted; they are won." The purpose of the Open Media Series, and of Chomsky's work, is to encourage readers to use their rights for creating greater justice, human rights, democracy, and to insist on a media system which supports them.

Foreword

by Peter Hart

There are any number of ways to study the mass media—comparing what is reported to what is neglected or buried in the back pages, or analyzing the sources and experts who dominate discussions of important events. Doing that sort of work helps to measure the distance from the rhetoric of media executives and superstar pundits to what appears on the printed page or TV screen. This gap between the values that corporate media barons profess to cherish—a robust, skeptical and adversarial press—and the product they sell is often considerable, but in elite circles paying lip service to the most cherished principles of the First Amendment seems to count more than actually living up to its principles.

The commentary sections of newspapers are, unsurprisingly, no different. The pledge to deliver to readers free-ranging debate is repeated ad nauseam—"a wide range of voices and perspectives," according to one paper; "a diversity of opinions to stimulate and challenge the thinking of readers," at another. An academic paper described the section as a place "where public discourse, through the mediation of a service editor, can emerge unfettered." The *New York Times* aspired to a page that "reflected the major social, cultural and political debates of the day."

Most op-ed pages fall well short of these lofty goals, though the *Times'* mission statement gets close to describing what is really going on. In the elite papers—the ones with the largest circulations which wield the most influence among the power-ful (primarily the *Los Angeles Times*, *Washington Post* and *New York Times*)—the op-ed page serves as one more place where the parameters of acceptable debate are clearly delineated. That which can be published regularly is obviously within these boundaries, and the ideas that never or rarely appear most cer-tainly do not. So the *Times* can say without exaggeration that their page, and many others like it, "reflects" a certain type of public debate—namely, the one that the elite political classes and corporate interests will tolerate. The debate that happens in official Washington might not much resemble the actual public debate on important issues, but it's the one that suppos-edly matters, and hence is the one that appears in the newspaper. The related field of television punditry—the hand-ful of journalists and commentators who make a living offering pithy sound bites about almost any subject—suffers, by no acci-dent, from the same very limited spectrum, often relying on the very same people to provide opinion and analysis.

The op-ed page and the syndicated column are not particu-larly new features of the mass media, though their exact history is somewhat murky. The *New York Times* credits itself for com-ing up with the now-familiar format in 1970: a page opposite the paper's own editorials—hence the name "op-ed"—that would mostly feature pieces submitted by writers from outside the paper. As is often the case in the world of elite journalism, other major papers followed the *Times*' lead, and the page became relatively common around the country.

While the *Times* might be considered responsible for mak-ing the format more popular, it seems unlikely that the paper had, in its own humble estimation, "given birth to a new baby called the Op-Ed page." (That was a self-assessment the *Times* made in 1990, under the modest headline "All the Views That

Are Fit to Print.") Scholars David Croteau and Bill Hoynes pointed out in Fairness & Accuracy in Reporting's (FAIR) magazine *Extra!* (June 1992) that syndicated political and economic columns were appearing in the 1920s; another study found newspapers around the country claim their own op-ed sections predated that of the *Times*.

More important than who "birthed" the format is what they did with it. While a freewheeling, broad debate sure sounds nice, this wasn't what was appearing in the *Times*. Former *Times* columnist Anthony Lewis, for example, once explained that the page was clearly a creature of the *Times*' own establishment-friendly politics, and the idea that he represented a left or progressive viewpoint that might balance the likes of William Safire was absurd. When Ben Bagdikian surveyed the opinion pages in the mid-1960s, he found that editors' claims that they sought out a wide ideological range of columnists was difficult to square with the fact that the papers had "a preponderance of conservative columnists."

Surveying the terrain nearly thirty years later, Croteau and Hoynes found a similar rightward skew in the distribution of political columnists. Of the top seven most-circulated columnists, four were well-known conservatives (George Will, James Kilpatrick, William Safire, and William F. Buckley). Rounding out the top tier were centrist political reporter David Broder and columnist Mike Royko, with Ellen Goodman as the lone liberal. As Croteau and Hoynes concluded, "The most widely distributed columnists of the day still deliver messages that resonate with the right, and there is still no coherent presentation of the 'other point of view.'"

About ten years later, another survey by FAIR found much the same—the ideological spectrum had hardly changed, but some names had shifted places. Archconservatives James Dobson and Cal Thomas were at the top of the list (calculated by the number of papers carrying their column), with fellow conservatives Robert Novak and George Will not far behind.

There have always been, of course, some exceptions to the rule. Populist progressive Molly Ivins, for example, was being carried in over 300 newspapers up until she passed away in early 2007. But in a broad sense, the opinion pages of daily newspapers are yet another corner of the corporate media universe where right-wing voices dominate, and the general debate extends from the far-right to the center, occasional exceptions notwithstanding.

This hardly seems open to serious debate, no matter what the most conservative pundits and cable news hosts have to say about the allegedly left-wing tendencies of the corporate press. Adam Meyerson, the editor of the newsletter of the conservative think tank Heritage Foundation, once explained (November 1988):

> Today, op-ed pages are dominated by conservatives. We have a tremendous amount of conservative opinion, but this creates a problem for those who are interested in a career in journalism after college. . . . If Bill Buckley were to come out of Yale today, nobody would pay much attention to him. He would not be that unusual . . . because there are probably hundreds of people with those ideas [and] they already have syndicated columns.

Young conservatives pining for their shot at the big-time commentary pages needn't lose all hope. In 1995, the president of The New York Times Syndicate noted that while there were "very few competitive markets left and fewer newspapers," there was still room for some things—particularly "conservative columns by minorities or women."

Meyerson's lament is nonetheless borne out by taking a glance at the Web sites for the major newspaper syndicates. If an op-ed page editor even truly desired to present left-leaning commentary to readers, it would be difficult to do so by relying on the major syndicates. One of the largest, Creators, offers at least two dozen well-known conservatives; genuine left or progressive writers can be counted on one hand.

And that's only part of the story. Over the last dozen years or so, major newspapers have jettisoned the few left-leaning opinion writers who have cracked into the elite media. In July 1995, *USA Today* fired its only progressive columnist, Barbara Reynolds. Two years later, the *Washington Post* dumped its one consistent voice for peace and justice, Colman McCarthy, who had written for the paper since the late '60s. The reason? "The market has spoken," according to *Post* managing editor Robert Kaiser. The paper would continue to find a "market" for the likes of far-right stalwarts like Charles Krauthammer and George Will, whose views seem to never require validation in the marketplace, no matter how out of step they might be with the public sentiment.

In 2005, the *Los Angeles Times* dropped left-leaning columnist Robert Scheer, a fixture at the paper for nearly thirty years. With the Iraq War the defining political issue of his final years as a *Times* columnist, Scheer was rare among mainstream pundits for being resolutely skeptical of White House claims about Iraq. Before it became convenient for media bigfoots to claim that "everyone" was wrong about Iraq's weapons of mass destruction, Scheer was writing (August 6, 2002) that "a consensus of experts" told the Senate that Iraq's chemical and biological arsenals were "almost totally destroyed during eight years of inspections."

Months later, Scheer would call the White House pretexts for war a "big lie." Scheer called for troop withdrawals from Iraq in late 2003, a position that would still be almost absent from elite discussion three years later. Scheer's firing could have been attributed to any number of factors: a right-wing campaign against him by the likes of Fox's Bill O'Reilly, or the paper shifting into the hands of the Tribune Company. Scheer himself said that the new publisher of the *Times* had told him that "he hated every word that I wrote."

With the paper dropping its best-known progressive writer, the *Times* beefed up its offerings from the right side of the political spectrum: neoconservative Max Boot, historian Niall Ferguson and Jonah Goldberg of the *National Review*. Some of Goldberg's notable contributions to the public debate had included deriding the French as "cheese-eating surrender monkeys" for opposing the Iraq War, and attempting to bait an academic critic of the Iraq occupation into betting $1,000 that there would be no civil war in Iraq and that most Americans and Iraqis would think the war "worth" it by early 2007.

It is unlikely that Goldberg—or any other conservatives with lofty perches in the corporate media—suffers many restless nights anxious about his job security in the allegedly left-wing media. One of the benefits of right-wing punditry is never having to worry much about the adverse consequences of being wrong about something (or, in some cases, many things). In 1992, for example, widely syndicated columnist George Will completely misrepresented the findings of a Gallup Poll in order to lambast Al Gore's views on global warming, arguing that most scientists did not believe warming was occurring. Gallup actually released a statement correcting Will's egregious error—their poll had found the opposite of what Will had written—but most of Will's readers never saw it, and Will never corrected his distortion.

Factual errors are one thing, but more often the pronouncements and prescriptions emanating from major pundits have other problems. *New York Times* foreign affairs columnist Tom Friedman has made a career out of offering simple-minded platitudes about globalization and the triumphant entrepreneurial zeal of corporate CEOs—that is, when not banging the drums for war and exhorting the United States to wage violence on people living in weaker states. Friedman nonetheless enjoys an undeserved reputation as one of the smartest minds in journalism (an astonishing fact given his work, but relative to his fellow columnists and pundits it is perhaps less shocking). In a 2006 discussion with NBC host Tim Russert, Friedman admitted that he knows little about one of the subjects to which he devotes significant time. Recalling a question he once fielded about whether he would ever oppose any so-called "free trade" agreement, Friedman recounted his answer: "No, absolutely not. . . . I wrote a column supporting the CAFTA, the Caribbean Free Trade initiative. I didn't even know what was in it. I just knew two words: free trade." It's worth noting that Friedman didn't even manage to call his favored trade agreement by its correct name; "CA" stands for Central American, not Caribbean.

The elite consensus on issues like trade means that widely-read columnists like Friedman need only to repeat the theology of globalization's many virtues in order to sound well-informed. Readers are unlikely to come across much that might challenge this orthodoxy, since within the corporate media's narrow spectrum of debate there is little disagreement.

It's useful to compare that consensus to public opinion, which has long been skeptical of trade deals like the North American

Free Trade Agreement (NAFTA). Citizen opposition to elite-friendly global trade policy is hardly considered a legitimate point of view. In 2000, mass movements against neoliberal prescriptions of the World Bank and International Monetary Fund (IMF) brought tens of thousands of activists to Washington, D.C.—and the scorn of opinion writers in the *New York Times*.

In less than a month, the *Times* ran five op-eds critical of the protests, and none that supported it, or even treated its concerns respectfully. That much seemed clear from the headlines ("Saving the Lost World," "Learning to Love the I.M.F.," and "A Real Nut Case"), but the pieces were more hysterical than their titles. Right-wing pundit (and soon-to-be White House speechwriter) David Frum claimed the protesters "hate dams and airports and economists." Critics of World Bank/IMF policies, according to *Times* columnist Paul Krugman, spouted "rarely fact-checked" arguments that represented "a small, relatively privileged minority." *Times*man Thomas Friedman, not one to be outdone on his home turf, angrily concluded that the demonstrators were "contemptible," a group of "economic quacks" who deserved to be labeled "The Coalition to Keep the World's Poor People Poor" and given "the back of your hand." Opposing voices only existed for the *Times* as objects of elitist scorn.

There are other historical moments where a careful analysis of op-eds provides a useful snapshot of the permissible discourse. In the month after the 9/11 attacks, for example, FAIR counted forty-four columns in the *Washington Post* and *New York Times* urging a military response; just two argued for non-military alternatives. While public surveys at the time showed a tilt towards some form of military action, there was considerable opinion that weighed towards limited attacks or using the international justice system to bring those responsible for the 9/11 attacks to account. (That this point of view would go largely unheard means it was not something to be taken seriously in elite political circles.) Years earlier, in his book *Necessary Illusions*, Noam Chomsky studied the spectrum of permitted debate over Nicaragua policy. He found that of the eighty-five columns appearing in the *New York Times* and *Washington Post* during the first three months of 1986, *all* were critical of the Sandinistas. More debate was allowed on the policy question of funding the Contras, which reflected the political debate in Washington. But denouncing the Sandinistas seemed to be a media requirement.

By almost any measure, the lack of diversity on the nation's op-ed pages is stunning. The issue of gender diversity, to take just one example, became a matter of public debate when author/pundit Susan Estrich took the *Los Angeles Times* to task for publishing a paltry number of op-eds written by women. The editor of the page, Michael Kinsley, shook his head at the mathematical difficulties of any attempt to broaden the debate and on March 20, 2005 wrote in the *Los Angeles Times*:

> If pressure for more women succeeds—as it will—there will be fewer black voices, fewer Latinos, and so on. Why should this be so? Aren't there black women and conservative Latinos? Of course there are. There may even be a wonderfully articulate disabled Latina lesbian conservative who is undiscovered because she is outside the comfortable old-boy network. But there probably aren't two. It's not a question of effort, it's mathematics. Each variable added to the equation subverts efforts to maximize all the other variables.

That sort of thinking is unfortunately common. Writing in the *New York Times* in 1990, Anna Quindlen recalled that one editor had told her, "I'd love to run your column, but we already run Ellen Goodman"—presumably one female writer was all the page could handle. African-American *Chicago Tribune* columnist Clarence Page reported that his syndicate often heard similar responses about his own work—editors would name black writers whose work was already appearing in their papers.

It might be useful, then, to read the columns collected in this volume against this historical backdrop. Unlike the Beltway soothsayers and pundits who are fixtures on TV chat shows, Noam Chomsky's writings are not informed by the whispers of anonymous officials, the chatter at Beltway watering holes or small talk at Donald Rumsfeld's Christmas party (yes, there is such a thing, and it has apparently been well-attended by the media elite in past years). These columns rely on the summoning of available facts—often inconvenient ones for the ruling classes, and therefore largely ignored by professional reporters—and on the words and deeds of powerful officials. It is exactly the sort of work that would exclude you from the corridors of power—a major sin in the world of elite journalism, if not a perfect way to lose your job.

It also might be useful—or frustrating—to try to imagine these columns appearing in your local newspaper on a fairly regular schedule. The likelihood of that happening might land somewhere between impossible and unimaginable. So the question, then, is why? Some years ago Noam Chomsky appeared on the flagship PBS newscast, the *MacNeil/Lehrer NewsHour*. In the pages of FAIR's magazine *Extra!*, a headline soon after read: "Chomsky Appears on MacNeil/Lehrer; Western Civilization Survives."

It did. But instead of the mere survival of American democracy, one might hope to see it flourish. Without expanding the ideas available to the mass public, that is impossible.

With a White House in all manner of disarray and George W. Bush enjoying historically low job approval ratings, critical assessments of White House policies are more commonplace in the corporate media. Still, this apparent openness can be illusory. Speaking on Pacifica's *Democracy Now!* on April 3, 2006, Chomsky sized up American media performance on the Iraq War at a time when the press was starting to get credit for finally expressing skepticism:

> There is virtually no criticism of the war in Iraq. Now, that will surprise journalists, I suppose. They think they're being very critical, but they're not. I mean, the kinds of criticism of the war in Iraq that are allowed in the doctrinal system, media and so on, are the kind of criticisms you heard about, say, in the German general staff after Stalingrad: it's not working; it's costing too much; we made a mistake, we should get a different general; something like that. In fact, it's about at the level of a high school newspaper cheering the local football team. You don't ask, "Should they win?" You ask, "How are we doing?" You know, "Did the coaches make a mistake? Should we try something else?" That's called criticism. . . . You know, the issue isn't how they are going to win, it's what are they doing there in the first place?

Journalists, writers, and political pundits whose opinions are acceptable to elite interests, and thus deemed fit to share their views on the most prestigious media stages, know to stay within these boundaries. The columns in this collection obey no such rules, and thus have stayed off the pages of the nation's elite newspapers. Like many things that are worth knowing, we are forced to read them elsewhere.

9/11: Lessons Unlearned

SEPTEMBER 4, 2002

September 11 shocked many Americans into an awareness that they had better pay much closer attention to what the U.S. government does in the world and how it is perceived. Many issues have been opened for discussion that were not on the agenda before. That's all to the good. It is also the merest sanity, if we hope to reduce the likelihood of future atrocities. It may be comforting to pretend that our enemies "hate our freedoms," as President Bush stated, but it is hardly wise to ignore the real world, which conveys different lessons.

The president is not the first to ask, "Why do they hate us?" In a staff discussion forty-four years ago, President Eisenhower described "the campaign of hatred against us [in the Arab world] not by the governments but by the people." His National Security Council outlined the basic reasons: The U.S. supports corrupt and oppressive governments and is "opposing political or economic progress" because of its interest in controlling the oil resources of the region.

Post-9/11 surveys in the Arab world reveal that the same reasons hold today, compounded with resentment over specific policies. Strikingly, that is even true of privileged, Western-oriented sectors in the region. To cite just one recent example: In the August 1 (2002) issue of the *Far Eastern Economic Review*, the internationally recognized regional specialist Ahmed Rashid writes that in Pakistan, "there is growing anger that U.S.

support is allowing (Musharraf's) military regime to delay the promise of democracy."

Today we do ourselves few favors by choosing to believe that "they hate us" and "hate our freedoms." On the contrary, these are attitudes of people who like Americans and admire much about the United States, including its freedoms. What they hate is official policies that deny them the freedoms to which they, too, aspire.

For such reasons, the post-9/11 rantings of Osama bin Laden—for example, about U.S. support for corrupt and brutal regimes, or about the U.S. "invasion" of Saudi Arabia—have a certain resonance, even among those who despise and fear him. From resentment, anger, and frustration, terrorist bands hope to draw support and recruits.

We should also be aware that much of the world regards Washington as a terrorist regime. In recent years, the United States has taken or backed actions in Colombia, Central America, Panama, Sudan and Turkey, to name only a few, that meet official U.S. definitions of "terrorism"—or worse—that is, when Americans apply the term to enemies.

In the most sober Establishment journal, *Foreign Affairs*, Samuel Huntington wrote in 1999, "While the United States regularly denounces various countries as 'rogue states,' in the eyes of many countries it is becoming the rogue superpower . . . the single greatest external threat to their societies."

Such perceptions are not changed by the fact that, on September 11, for the first time, a Western country was subjected on home soil to a horrendous terrorist attack of a kind all too familiar to victims of Western power. The attack goes far beyond what's sometimes called the "retail terror" of the IRA, FLN, or Red Brigade.

The September 11 terrorism elicited harsh condemnation

throughout the world and an outpouring of sympathy for the innocent victims. But with qualifications. An international Gallup Poll in late September 2001 found little support for "a military attack" by the United States in Afghanistan. The least support came from Latin America, the region with the most experience of U.S. intervention (2 percent in Mexico, for example).

The current "campaign of hatred" in the Arab world is, of course, also fueled by U.S. policies toward Israel-Palestine and Iraq. The United States has provided the crucial support for Israel's harsh military occupation, now in its thirty-fifth year.

One way to lessen Israeli-Palestinian tensions would be to stop increasing them, as we do, by not only refusing to join the long-standing international consensus that calls for recognition of the right of all states in the region to live in peace and security, including a Palestinian state in the currently occupied territories (perhaps with minor and mutual border adjustments), but also by providing the crucial economic, military, diplomatic and ideological support for Israel's unremitting efforts to render such an outcome unattainable.

In Iraq, a decade of harsh sanctions under U.S. pressure has strengthened Saddam Hussein while leading to the death of hundreds of thousands of Iraqis—perhaps more people "than have been slain by all so-called weapons of mass destruction throughout history," military analysts John and Karl Mueller wrote in *Foreign Affairs* in 1999.

Washington's present justifications for attacking Iraq have far less credibility than when President Bush I was welcoming Saddam as an ally and a trading partner, well after he had committed his worst crimes—the Halabja gassing, the al-Anfal massacres, and others. At the time, the murderer Saddam, strongly backed by Washington and London, was more dangerous than he is today.

As for a U.S. attack against Iraq, no one, including Donald Rumsfeld, can realistically guess the possible costs and consequences.

Radical Islamist extremists surely hope that an attack on Iraq will kill many people and destroy much of the country, providing recruits for terrorist actions.[1] They presumably also welcome the "Bush doctrine" that proclaims the right of attack against potential threats, which are virtually limitless. The president has announced that "There's no telling how many wars it will take to secure freedom in the homeland." That's true.

Threats are everywhere, even at home. The prescription for endless war poses a far greater danger to Americans than perceived enemies do, for reasons the terrorist organizations understand very well.

Twenty years ago, the former head of Israeli military intelligence, Yehoshaphat Harkabi, also a leading Arabist, made a point that still holds true. "To offer an honorable solution to the Palestinians respecting their right to self-determination: That is the solution of the problem of terrorism," he said. "When the swamp disappears, there will be no more mosquitos."

At the time, Israel enjoyed the virtual immunity from retaliation within the occupied territories that lasted until very recently. But Harkabi's warning was apt, and the lesson applies more generally.

Well before 9/11 it was understood that with modern technology, the rich and powerful will lose their near monopoly of the means of violence and can expect to suffer atrocities on home soil.

If we insist on creating more swamps, there will be more mosquitos, with awesome capacity for destruction.

If we devote our resources to draining the swamps, addressing the roots of the "campaigns of hatred," not only can we reduce the threats we face but we can also live up to ideals that we profess and that are not beyond reach if we choose to take them seriously.

NOTES

1. Expressing the standard view of intelligence analysts, Michael Scheuer, senior intelligence analyst in charge of tracking bin Laden from 1996, writes in his book *Imperial Hubris* (2004) that "there is nothing bin Laden could have hoped for more than the American invasion and occupation of Iraq, [which is] Osama bin Laden's gift from America." In *Journey of the Jihadist* (2006), the most detailed scholarly work on the jihadi movements, Fawaz Gerges reviews how the 9/11 terrorist crimes had been harshly condemned by jihadis, offering the U.S. an opportunity to split them from bin Laden. But Bush's quick resort to violence, and particularly the invasion of Iraq, welded them together, in the end creating a much more serious terrorist threat.

The United States versus Iraq:
A Modest Proposal

NOVEMBER 1, 2002

The dedicated efforts of the Bush administration to take control of Iraq—by war, military coup or some other means—have elicited various analyses of the guiding motives.

Offering one interpretation, Anatol Lieven, senior associate of the Carnegie Endowment for International Peace, in Washington, D.C., observes that the Bush efforts conform to "the classic modern strategy of an endangered right-wing oligarchy, which is to divert mass discontent into nationalism" through fear of external enemies. The administration's goal, Lieven says, is "unilateral world domination through absolute military superiority," which is why much of the world is so frightened and antagonistic towards the U.S. government—often misdescribed as "anti-Americanism."

Lieven's interpretation is supported, and can be extended, by an examination of the antecedents of Washington's bellicosity.

Ever since the September 11 attacks, Republicans have used the terrorist threat as a pretext to accelerate their right-wing political agenda. For the congressional elections, the strategy has diverted attention from the economy to war. When the presidential campaign begins, Republicans surely do not want people to be asking questions about their pensions, jobs, health care and other matters. Rather, they should be praising their heroic leader for rescuing them from imminent destruction by a foe of colossal power, and marching on to confront the next powerful force bent on our destruction.

The September 11 atrocities also provided an opportunity and pretext to implement long-standing plans to take control of Iraq's immense oil wealth, a central component of the Persian Gulf resources that the State Department, in 1945, described as a "stupendous source of strategic power, and one of the greatest material prizes in world history." Control of energy sources fuels U.S. economic and military might, and "strategic power" translates to a lever of world control.

A different interpretation is that the administration believes exactly what it says: Iraq has suddenly become a threat to our very existence and to its neighbors. So we must ensure that Iraq's weapons of mass destruction and the means for producing them are destroyed, and Saddam Hussein, the monster himself, eliminated. And quickly. The war must be waged this winter (2002/2003). Next winter will be too late. By then the mushroom cloud that National Security Adviser Condoleezza Rice predicts may have already consumed us.

Let us assume that this interpretation is correct. If the powers in the Middle East fear Washington more than Saddam, as they apparently do, that just reveals their limited grasp of reality. And it is only an accident that by next winter the U.S. presidential campaign will be under way.

Adopting the official interpretation, we then face the obvious question: "How can we achieve the announced goals?" On these assumptions, we see at once that the administration has overlooked a simple alternative to invading Iraq. Let Iran do it. That simple plan seems to have been ignored, perhaps because it would be regarded as insane, and rightly so. But it is instructive to ask why.

The modest proposal, then, is for the United States to encourage Iran to invade Iraq, providing the Iranians with the necessary logistical and military support, from a safe distance (missiles, bombs, bases, etc.). As a proxy, one pole of "the axis of evil" would take on another.

The proposal has many advantages over the alternatives.

First, Saddam will be overthrown—in fact, torn to shreds along with anyone close to him. His weapons of mass destruction will also be destroyed, along with the means to produce them.

Second, there will be no American casualties. True, many Iraqis and Iranians will die. But that can hardly be a concern. The Bush circles—many of them recycled Reaganites—strongly supported Saddam after he attacked Iran in 1980, quite oblivious to the enormous human cost, either then or under the subsequent sanctions regime.

Saddam is likely to use chemical weapons. But the current leadership firmly backed the "Beast of Baghdad" when he used chemical weapons against Iran in the Reagan years, and when he used gas against "his own people," to repeat the standard refrain: Kurds, who were his own people in the sense that Cherokees were Andrew Jackson's people.[1]

The current Washington planners continued to support the Beast after he had committed by far his worst crimes, even providing him with means to develop weapons of mass destruction, nuclear and biological, right up to the invasion of Kuwait.

Bush I and Cheney also effectively authorized Saddam's slaughter of Shiites in March 1991, in the interests of "stability," as was soberly explained at the time. They withdrew their support for his attack on the Kurds only under great international and domestic pressure.

Third, the UN will be no problem. It will be unnecessary to explain to the world that the UN is relevant when it follows U.S. orders, otherwise not.

Fourth, Iran surely has far better credentials for war-making, and for running a post-Saddam Iraq, than Washington. Unlike the Bush administration, Iran has no record of support for the murderous Saddam and his program of weapons of mass destruction.

One might object, correctly, that we cannot trust the Iranian leadership, but surely that is even more true of those who continued to aid Saddam well after his worst crimes.

Furthermore, we will be spared the embarrassment of professing blind faith in our leaders in the manner that we justly ridicule in totalitarian states.

Fifth, the liberation will be greeted with enthusiasm by much of the population, far more so than if Americans invade. People will cheer on the streets of Basra and Karbala, and we can join Iranian journalists in hailing the nobility and just cause of the liberators.

Sixth, Iran can move toward instituting "democracy." The majority of the population is Shiite, and Iran would have fewer problems than the United States in granting them some say in a successor government.

There will be no problem in gaining access to Iraqi oil, just as U.S. companies could easily exploit Iranian energy resources right now, if Washington would permit it.

Granted, the modest proposal that Iran liberate Iraq is insane. Its only merit is that it is far more reasonable than the plans now being implemented—or it would be, if the administration's professed goals had any relation to the real ones.

NOTES

1. As it turned out, Saddam did not have chemical weapons in 2003. But it was plausibly assumed that he did, which is why U.S. troops were equipped with protective devices, serious precautions were taken in Israel, etc.

The Case Against the War in Iraq

MARCH 3, 2003

The most powerful state in history has proclaimed that it intends to control the world by force, the dimension in which it reigns supreme. President Bush and his cohorts evidently believe that the means of violence in their hands are so extraordinary that they can dismiss with contempt anyone who stands in their way.

The consequences could be catastrophic in Iraq and around the world. The United States may reap a whirlwind of terrorist retaliation—and step up the possibility of nuclear Armageddon.

Bush, Cheney, Rumsfeld, and company are committed to an "imperial ambition," as John Ikenberry wrote in the September/October (2002) issue of *Foreign Affairs*—"a unipolar world in which the United States has no peer competitor" and in which "no state or coalition could ever challenge it as global leader, protector and enforcer." That ambition surely includes much-expanded control over Persian Gulf resources and military bases to impose a preferred form of order in the region.

Even before the administration began beating the war drums against Iraq, there were plenty of warnings that U.S. adventurism would lead to proliferation of weapons of mass destruction, as well as terror, for deterrence or revenge.

Right now, Washington is teaching the world a very ugly and dangerous lesson: If you want to defend yourself from us, you had better mimic North Korea and pose a credible military threat. Otherwise we will demolish you.

There is good reason to believe that the war with Iraq is intended, in part, to demonstrate what lies ahead when the empire decides to strike a blow—though "war" is hardly the proper term, given the gross mismatch of forces.

A flood of propaganda warns that if we do not stop Saddam Hussein today he will destroy us tomorrow. Last October (2002), when Congress granted the president the authority to go to war, it was "to defend the national security of the United States against the continuing threat posed by Iraq."

But no country in Iraq's neighborhood seems overly concerned about Saddam, much as they may hate the murderous tyrant. Perhaps that is because the neighbors know that Iraq's people are at the edge of survival. Iraq has become one of the weakest states in the region. As a report from the American Academy of Arts and Sciences points out, Iraq's economy and military expenditures are a fraction even of Kuwait's, with 10 percent of Iraq's population.

Indeed, in recent years, countries nearby have sought to reintegrate Iraq into the region, including Iran and Kuwait, both invaded by Iraq.

Saddam benefited from U.S. support through the war with Iran and beyond, up to the day of the invasion of Kuwait. Those responsible are largely back at the helm in Washington today. Reagan and the previous Bush administration provided aid to Saddam, along with the means to develop weapons of mass destruction, back when Saddam was far more dangerous than he is now and had already committed his worst crimes, like murdering thousands of Kurds with poison gas.

An end to Saddam's rule would lift a horrible burden from the people of Iraq. There is good reason to believe that he would have suffered the fate of Ceausescu and other vicious tyrants backed by the U.S.-U.K. if Iraqi society had not been devastated by harsh sanctions that force the population to rely on Saddam for survival while strengthening him and his clique.

Saddam remains a terrible threat to those within his reach. Today, his reach does not extend beyond his own domains, though it is likely that U.S. aggression could inspire a new generation of terrorists bent on revenge, and might induce Iraq to carry out terrorist actions suspected to be already in place.

Last year (2002) a task force chaired by Gary Hart and Warren Rudman prepared a report for the Council on Foreign Relations, "America—Still Unprepared, Still in Danger." It warns of likely terrorist attacks that could be far worse than 9/11, including possible use of weapons of mass destruction (WMD) in this country, dangers that become "more urgent by the prospect of the United States' going to war with Iraq."

Right now Saddam has every reason to keep under tight control any chemical and biological weapons that Iraq may have. He wouldn't provide such weapons to the Osama bin Ladens of the world, who represent a terrible threat to Saddam himself, quite apart from the reaction if there is even a hint that such a deadly transaction might take place. And administration hawks understand that, except as a last resort if attacked, Iraq is highly unlikely to use any weapons of mass destruction that it has—and risk instant incineration.

Under attack, however, Iraqi society would collapse, including the controls over any weapons of mass destruction. These could be "privatized," as international security specialist Daniel Benjamin warns, and offered to the huge "market for unconventional weapons, where they will have no trouble finding buyers." That really is "a nightmare scenario," he says.[1]

As for the fate of the people of Iraq in war, no one can predict with any confidence: not the CIA, not Rumsfeld, not those who claim to be experts on Iraq, no one. But international relief agencies are preparing for the worst.

Studies by respected medical organizations estimate that the death toll could rise to the hundreds of thousands. Confidential UN documents warn that a war could trigger a "humanitarian emergency of exceptional scale"—including the possibility that 30 percent of Iraqi children could die from malnutrition.[2]

Today the administration doesn't seem to be heeding the international relief agency warnings about an attack's horrendous aftermath.

The potential disasters are among the many reasons why decent human beings do not contemplate the threat or use of violence, whether in personal life or international affairs, unless reasons have been offered that have overwhelming force. And surely nothing remotely like that justification has come forward.

NOTES

1. Apparently, something like the "nightmare scenario" occurred. There were indeed means to develop weapons of mass destruction in Iraq: under guard by UN inspectors, who were dismantling them, and who had to be withdrawn when the United States invaded. Rumsfeld, Wolfowitz and associates neglected to instruct their forces to secure these sites. The UN inspectors continued their work by satellite and reported that over one-hundred sites were systematically looted, including lethal biotoxins and precision equipment usable for missiles and nuclear weapons. Destination unknown, and not pleasant to contemplate.

2. The most authoritative study of casualties to date, prepared with the cooperation of the Massachusetts Institute of Technology (MIT) Center for International Studies, is Gilbert Burnham et al., "The Human Cost of the War in Iraq," *Lancet*, October 2006. It estimates the most probable toll of post-invasion excess deaths at 650,000. In addition there are millions of refugees and vast destruction and misery.

Now That the War Has Begun

MARCH 24, 2003

If anything is obvious from the history of warfare, it's that very little can be predicted.

In Iraq, the most awesome military force in human history has attacked a much weaker country—an enormous disparity of force. It will be some time before even preliminary assessments of the consequences can be made. Every effort must be dedicated to minimizing the harm, and to providing the Iraqi people with the huge resources that are required for them to rebuild their society, post-Saddam—in their own way, not as dictated by foreign rulers.

There is no reason to doubt the near-universal judgment that the war in Iraq will only increase the threat of terror and development and possible use of weapons of mass destruction, for revenge or deterrence.[1]

In Iraq the Bush administration is pursuing an "imperial ambition" that is, rightly, frightening the world and turning the United States into an international pariah. The avowed intent of current U.S. policy is to assert a military power that is supreme in the world, and beyond challenge. U.S. preventive wars may be fought at will—preventive, not preemptive. Whatever the justifications for preemptive war might sometimes be, they do not hold for the very different category of preventive war: the use of force to eliminate a perceived or contrived threat.

That policy opens the way to protracted struggle between the United States and its enemies, some of them created by violence and aggression, and not just in the Middle East. In that regard, the U.S. attack on Iraq is an answer to bin Laden's prayers.

For the world the stakes of the war and its aftermath almost couldn't be higher. To select just one of many possibilities, destabilization in Pakistan could lead to a turnover of "loose nukes" to the global network of terrorist groups, which may well be invigorated by the invasion and military occupation of Iraq. Other possibilities, no less grim, are easy to conjure up.

Yet the outlook for more benign outcomes isn't hopeless— starting with the world's support for the victims of war, brutal tyranny, and murderous sanctions in Iraq.

A promising sign is that opposition to the invasion, before and after the fact, has been entirely without precedent. By contrast, forty-one years ago this month (March 2003), when the Kennedy administration launched a direct attack against South Vietnam, protest was almost nonexistent. It did not reach any meaningful level for several years, when several hundred thousand troops were in South Vietnam, which had been devastated, and the U.S. had extended the war to the North.

Today there is large-scale, committed and principled popular antiwar protest all over the United States—and the world. The peace movement acted forcefully even before the new Iraq war started.

That reflects a steady increase over these years in unwillingness to tolerate aggression and atrocities, one of many such changes worldwide. The activist movements of the past forty years have had a civilizing effect.

By now, the only way for the United States to attack a much weaker enemy is to construct a huge propaganda offensive depicting it as the ultimate evil—or even as a threat to our very survival. That was Washington's scenario for Iraq.[2]

Nevertheless, peace activists are in a much better position now to stop the next turn to violence, and that is a matter of extraordinary significance.

A large part of the opposition to Bush's war is based on recognition that Iraq is only a special case of the "imperial ambition" declared forcefully in last September's (2002) National Security Strategy.

For perspective on our current situation, it may be useful to attend to very recent history. Last October (2002) the nature of threats to peace was dramatically underscored at the summit meeting in Havana on the fortieth anniversary of the Cuban Missile Crisis, attended by key participants from Cuba, Russia, and the United States.

The fact that we survived the crisis was a miracle. We learned that the world was saved from possible nuclear devastation by one Russian submarine captain, Vasily Arkhipov, who countermanded an order to fire nuclear-tipped torpedos when Russian submarines were attacked by U.S. destroyers near Kennedy's "quarantine" line. Had Arkhipov agreed, the nuclear launch would almost certainly have set off an interchange that could have "destroy[ed] the Northern hemisphere," as Eisenhower had warned.

The dreadful revelation is particularly timely because of the circumstances: The roots of the missile crisis lay in international terrorism aimed at "regime change," two top-of-mind concepts today. U.S. terrorist attacks against Cuba began shortly after Castro took power, and were sharply escalated by Kennedy, right up to the missile crisis and beyond.

The new discoveries demonstrate with brilliant clarity the terrible and unanticipated risks of attacks on a "much weaker enemy" aimed at "regime change"—risks that could doom us all, it is no exaggeration to say.

The United States is forging new and dangerous paths over near-unanimous world opposition.

There are two ways for Washington to respond to the threats that are, in part, engendered by its actions and startling proclamations.

One way is to try to alleviate the threats by paying some attention to legitimate grievances, and by agreeing to become a civilized member of a world community, with some respect for world order and its institutions.

The other way is to construct even more awesome instruments of destruction and domination, so that any perceived challenge, however remote, can be crushed—provoking new and greater challenges.

NOTES

1. Postwar intelligence assessments revealed that the increase was well beyond what had been anticipated. See my *Failed States* (2006), page 18ff., and the classified National Intelligence Estimate, reported by Mark Mazzetti, "Spy Agencies Say Iraq War Worsens Terrorism Threat," in the *New York Times*, September 24, 2006. In the March/April 2007 issue of *Mother Jones*, terrorism specialists Peter Bergen and Paul Cruickshank discussed their recent study showing that "the Iraq War has generated a stunning sevenfold increase in the yearly rate of fatal jihadist attacks, amounting to literally hundreds of additional terrorist attacks and thousands of civilian lives lost; even when terrorism in Iraq and Afghanistan is excluded, fatal attacks in the rest of the world have increased by more than one-third."

2. Policy makers are aware of the problem. A leaked document of the incoming Bush I administration, reviewing "third world threats," concluded that "in cases where the U.S. confronts much weaker enemies"—the only ones it makes sense to fight—"our challenge will be not simply to defeat them, but to defeat them decisively and rapidly." Any other course would be "embarrassing" and might "undercut political support," recognized to be thin. See Maureen Dowd, *New York Times*, March 2, 1991.

Iraq Is a Trial Run

APRIL 29, 2003

Amid the chaos that is now Iraq, the question of who rules the country remains the prime issue of contention: the Iraqis, or a clique in Crawford, Texas?

Unsurprisingly, leading secular and religious figures of the opposition to Saddam Hussein want Iraqis to control Iraq, with the United Nations as intermediary.

U.S. policymakers have a radically different conception. They appear to be committed to imposing a client regime in Iraq, following the practice elsewhere in the region and, most significantly, in the regions that have been under U.S. domination for a century: Central America and the Caribbean.

Brent Scowcroft, national security adviser to Bush I, has just repeated the obvious: "What's going to happen the first time we hold an election in Iraq and it turns out the radicals win? What do you do? We're surely not going to let them take over."

The region is profoundly skeptical about U.S. motives. From Morocco to Lebanon to the Gulf, close to 95 percent of the population believe that the Iraq war was waged to ensure "control of Arab oil and the subjugation of the Palestinians to Israel's will," said Youssef Ibrahim in the *Washington Post*, citing a survey commissioned by Shibley Telhami of the University of Maryland.

If experience is any guide, the Bush public relations team will want to put into place some kind of formal democracy in

Iraq, as long as it has little substance. It's hard to imagine that Washington would allow a real voice to the Shiite majority, which is likely to press for Islamic leadership and to try to establish closer relations with Iran, the last thing the Bushites want. Or that they would allow a real voice to the Kurdish minority, who are likely to seek some kind of autonomy within a federal structure that would be anathema to Turkey.

Turkey remains a major base for U.S. power—despite tensions over the fact that the Turkish government followed the will of its people in not allowing U.S. troops to invade Iraq from its territory.

Functioning democracy in the Middle East would have outcomes inconsistent with the U.S. goal of reinforcing its dominance there.

The Bush administration has publicly announced that the next targets could be Syria and Iran—which would require a strong military base in Iraq, presumably; another reason why any meaningful democracy is unlikely to be permitted there.

Military bases at the heart of the world's major energy resources also have obvious implications for solidifying control over these resources and the strategic power and material wealth they provide.

The Iraq war is a trial run to make it clear to the world that the Bush administration intends its National Security Strategy, announced last September (2002), to be taken seriously. The message was that the Bush administration intends to rule the world by force, the one dimension in which it reigns supreme, and to do so permanently, removing any potential challenge it receives. That is the heart of the newly announced doctrine of preventive war.

Before waging war against Iraq, the United States felt compelled to try to force the world to accept its position and could not. Usually, the world succumbs. Take the First Gulf War. There the United States applied considerable pressure to induce the Security Council to agree to its war plan, though much of the world opposed it. In any legal system that you take seriously, coerced judgments are considered invalid. But in the international affairs conducted by the powerful, coerced judgments are fine. They are called diplomacy.

The United Nations is now in a very hazardous position. The United States might move to dismantle it—or at least to diminish it. The extremist stand of the current administration endangers the organization severely and, along with it, the entire framework of international law that was painfully constructed after World War II as a foundation for a more peaceful world.

Of course it is important to maintain power at home as well. Last fall (2002), in the midterm elections, the Bush administration would have done poorly if social and economic issues had been at the forefront. Instead, it managed to emphasize security issues like the supposed threat of Iraq. By the time of the presidential election, the administration will have to find another dragon to slay.

Meanwhile, high on the agenda for American citizens should be to work to ensure that Iraq is run by Iraqis, and that the United States provides massive aid, to be used as the Iraqis themselves decide—quite likely for something other than U.S. taxpayer subsidies to Halliburton and Bechtel.

Another priority should be putting a brake on the extremely dangerous policies announced in the National Security Strategy, and carried out in the "petri dish" of Iraq, as David Sanger and Steven Weisman of the *New York Times* described it.

There should also be serious efforts to block the bonanza of arms sales that, happily anticipated as a consequence of the war, will contribute to making the world a more awful and dangerous place.

The agenda, as always, begins with trying to find out what is happening in the world, and then doing something about it, as we can, better than anyone else. Few share our privilege, power and freedom—hence responsibility. That should be another truism.

Road Map to Nowhere

AUGUST 18, 2003

Today, as the Israeli-Palestinian peace process continues, so does the building of the barrier that Israelis call a "security fence," and Palestinians, a "separation wall."[1]

President George W. Bush and Prime Minister Ariel Sharon may have differences of opinion about the barrier's exact location. But to put the peace process—and the barrier—in context, it is important to remember that without U.S. authorization and support, Israel can do very little. And sensible Israelis know it. Israeli political commentator Amir Oren was quite accurate in observing that "the boss-man called 'partner' is the U.S. administration."

There are many illusions in the Arab countries and elsewhere about Washington's subordination to Israel or to the pro-Israel domestic lobby (which isn't all Jewish by any means). The idea that the United States would let Israel boss it around is a serious misunderstanding, in my view.[2]

Israel's choices of the past thirty years have reduced its options considerably. On its present course, it has virtually no alternative to serving as a U.S. military base in the region and complying with U.S. demands.

The options were starkly illuminated in 1971, when President Sadat of Egypt offered Israel a full peace treaty in return for Israeli withdrawal from Egyptian territory, accepting the proposals of UN mediator Gunnar Jarring. Israel had a fateful choice: It could accept peace and integration into the region, or insist on expansion and confrontation, hence inevitable dependency on the United States. It chose the latter course, not on grounds of security, but because of a commitment to expansion, at the time, primarily into the Egyptian Sinai, which led directly to the 1973 war, a very close call for Israel, and for the world, as the great powers became involved. It is by no means unusual for states to rank security well below other goals, the United States included.

Last year (May 2002) in *Foreign Affairs* Hussein Agha, a Middle East scholar at Oxford University, and Robert Malley, a special assistant to President Clinton for Arab-Israeli affairs, observed of the Israeli-Palestinian impasse that "the outlines of a solution have been basically understood for some time now." Agha and Malley sketch the common understanding: a territorial divide on the international border, now with a 1-1 land swap. They write that "the way to get (to the solution) has eluded all sides from the start," but while accurate, the statement is misleading. The way has been blocked for twenty-five years by the United States, and Israel continues to reject it even at the dovish extreme of the dominant political spectrum.

During the Bush II-Sharon years, the prospects for a diplomatic solution have declined. Israel has expanded its settlement programs, with continued U.S. backing. Israeli settlements now control 42 percent of the West Bank, according to B'Tselem, the Israeli human-rights organization. Interspersed among those settlements are Palestinian areas that are "reminiscent of distasteful regimes from the past, such as the apartheid regime of South Africa," B'Tselem reports.[3]

As for current Bush administration plans, there are two sources of information: rhetoric and action. At the rhetorical level is Bush's "vision" of a Palestinian state—which we are to admire though not permitted to perceive—and the "road map" of the "quartet": the UN, Russia, EU, and the United States. But the "road map" was purposely left vague on many important issues, including even the core issue of boundaries. Furthermore, while Israel formally accepted the "road map," it immediately issued fourteen reservations that completely eviscerated it, with the support of the United States. Hence both Israel and the U.S. were at once in violation of the "road map" that is commonly though inaccurately described as a Bush administration initiative.[4]

"The facts on the ground," Israeli journalist Amira Hass comments, "are determining—and will continue to determine—the area where the road map will be applied, the area where the entity known as the 'Palestinian state' will be established."

With the barrier and by its other actions, Israel—and, by extension, its "boss-man called 'partner'"—undermine hopes for a peaceful diplomatic settlement, surely by design, since the consequences are so obvious.

Israel justifies its behavior in terms of Palestinian terror, which did indeed escalate, including the suicide bombings against Israeli civilians, during the al-Aqsa Intifada that broke out in September 2000. It must be noted, however, that until fairly recently, Israel's brutal military occupation elicited very little retaliation against Israel from within the territories, and crimes committed there by the occupying forces and the illegal settlers elicited little concern.

The same was true in the early days of the current Intifada. In its first month, according to the Israeli army, the ratio of killings was almost 20 to 1 (75 Palestinians, 4 Israelis), at a time when resistance was confined to the territories and rarely went much beyond stone throwing. It was only when the ratio shifted to closer to 3 to 1 that enormous indignation was aroused: over the suffering of innocent Israelis.

The reaction to the suffering of Israelis is proper. But has it been proper to disregard the far worse suffering of Palestinians before the balance of terror shifted, and today as well—suffering that goes back many years with crucial U.S. support?

The Intifada has exposed significant changes that had been taking place within Israel. The internal authority of the Israeli military by then had reached such levels that Israeli military correspondent Ben Kaspit describes the country as "not a state with an army, but an army with a state"; an army that is, furthermore, virtually an adjunct of the military force that dominates the world at a level beyond any historical precedent, a fact not lost on the people of the region.

Yet a just peace could come. There are many historical examples of the termination and reversal of seemingly intractable conflicts. Northern Ireland is a recent example; though no utopia, it is vastly improved over what it was a decade ago.

South Africa is another case. Only a few years ago, racial conflict and violent repression seemed to be driving the society to hopeless despair. There have been remarkable improvements since, though for the majority of the population, black and impoverished, conditions have scarcely improved, and for many may have worsened.

In Israel-Palestine, each day's wrenching horror adds new boulders to the walls of hatred, fear, and consuming desire for revenge. But it is never too late to breach those walls.

Only the people who suffer the daily pain and anticipate worse tomorrow can seriously undertake this task directly, but those outside can help substantially to ease the way, though not until they are willing to face honestly their own roles and responsibilities—and hammer out a meaningful road map accordingly, while compelling their governments to implement it.

NOTES

1. In 2004, the International Court of Justice declared the Israeli wall illegal. U.S. Justice Buergenthal issued a separate declaration agreeing that the Fourth Geneva Convention, which bars transfer of population from the conqueror to occupied territories, applies to the West Bank, so that "the segments of the wall being built by Israel to protect the settlements are *ipso facto* in violation of international humanitarian law" (International Court of Justice, July 9, 2004)—that is, 80–85 percent of the wall, clearly constructed to protect settlers, and in fact increasing the security threat to Israel unless all Palestinians are expelled from the areas illegally taken over within the wall. In May 2006 Israel's prime minister announced his "convergence" plan, which converts the wall to an annexation wall. The plan calls for Israel to take over the regions within the wall, to dismember the shrinking fragments left to Palestinians, and to imprison the fragments by taking over the Jordan Valley. It was supported by the Bush administration, and praised as "moderate" in Western commentary—perhaps too moderate, the U.S.-Israel determined after their invasion of Lebanon in July 2006.

2. Sometimes Washington has gone out of its way to humiliate Israel, with no reaction from the lobby. For one striking example in 2005, see *Failed States*, page 189. Uri Avnery argues that U.S. orders blocked Israel's plans for the 2006 Lebanon war, planned well in advance, Prime Minister Ehud Olmert

conceded in March 2007. Avnery, "Olmert's Truth," March 10, 2007, see http://www.avnery-news.co.il/english/. See also note 1 to "Dilemmas of Dominance" on page 48.

3. These numbers, incidentally, are mostly meaningless, because they do not take into account the projected borders of the settlements, mostly state secrets, or the huge infrastructure projects—superhighways for Israelis from which Palestinians are barred, with very wide borders; the Israeli checkpoints and other devices to make life impossible for Palestinians, etc. A realistic estimate would probably be that Israeli settlements now control about 70 percent of the West Bank, but there are no definite figures since neither the United States nor Israel will reveal the facts. For updates on Israeli settlements, see B'Tselem, or the regular *Report on Israeli Settlements* of the Foundation for Middle East Peace.

4. "Israeli Cabinet Statement on Road Map and 14 Reservations," May 25, 2003. Israel demanded that Palestinians must ensure full quiet and end of incitement, but "the Roadmap will not state that Israel must cease violence and incitement against the Palestinians." "Israel's right to exist as a Jewish state" must be affirmed and right of return waived, but UN affirmation of Palestinian rights is barred from discussion, along with Israeli settlements and much else. With U.S. approval of such conditions, the Road Map was dead on arrival. The first mainstream reference appears to be Jimmy Carter, *Palestine: Peace not Apartheid.*

9/11 and the "Age of Terror"

SEPTEMBER 2, 2003

Amid the aftershocks of suicide bombings in Baghdad, Jerusalem and Najaf, and countless other horrors since September 11, 2001, it is easy to understand why many believe that the world has entered a new and frightening "age of terror," the title of a recent collection of essays by Yale University scholars and others. However, two years after 9/11, the United States has yet to confront the roots of terrorism, has waged more war than peace and has continually raised the stakes of international confrontation.

On 9/11 the world reacted with shock and horror, and with sympathy for the victims. But it is important to bear in mind that for much of the world, there was a further reaction: "Welcome to the club." For the first time in history, a Western power was subjected to an atrocity of the kind that is all too familiar elsewhere.

Any attempt to make sense of events since 9/11 will naturally begin with an investigation of American power—how it has reacted and what course it may take.

Within a year of 9/11, Afghanistan was under attack. Those who accept elementary moral standards have some work to do to show that the United States and Britain were justified in bombing Afghans to compel them to turn over people suspected of criminal atrocities, the official reason given when the bombings began.[1]

Then in September 2002, the most powerful state in history announced a new National Security Strategy asserting that it will maintain global hegemony permanently. Any challenge will be blocked by force, the dimension in which the United States reigns supreme.

At the same time, the war drums began to beat to mobilize the population for an invasion of Iraq. And the campaign opened for the midterm congressional elections, which would determine whether the administration would be able to carry out its radical international and domestic agenda.

The final days of 2002, foreign-policy specialist Michael Krepon wrote, were "the most dangerous since the 1962 Cuban missile crisis," which Arthur Schlesinger described, reasonably, as "the most dangerous moment in human history." Krepon's concern was nuclear proliferation in "Iran, Iraq, North Korea and the Indian subcontinent," an "unstable nuclear-proliferation belt stretching from Pyongyang to Baghdad." Bush administration initiatives in 2002–2003 have only increased the threats in and near this unstable belt.

The National Security Strategy declared that the United States—alone—has the right to carry out "preventive war": preventive, not preemptive, using military force to eliminate a perceived threat, even if invented or imagined. Preventive war is, very simply, the "supreme crime" condemned at Nuremberg.

From early September (2002), the Bush administration issued grim warnings about the danger that Saddam Hussein posed to the United States, with broad hints that Saddam was linked to al-Qaeda and involved in the 9/11 attacks. The propaganda assault helped enable the administration to gain support from a frightened population for the planned invasion of a country known to be virtually defenseless, and a valuable prize, at the heart of the world's major energy system.

Last May (2003), after the putative end of the war in Iraq, President Bush landed on the deck of the aircraft carrier *Abraham Lincoln* and declared that he had won a "victory in the war on terror [by having] removed an ally of al-Qaida."

But September 11, 2003 will arrive with no credible evidence for the alleged link between Saddam and his bitter enemy Osama bin Laden. And the only known link between the victory and terror is that the U.S. invasion of Iraq seems to have increased al-Qaeda recruitment and the threat of terror.

The *Wall Street Journal* recognized that Bush's carefully staged *Abraham Lincoln* extravaganza "marks the beginning of his 2004 re-election campaign," which the White House hopes "will be built as much as possible around national-security themes." If the administration lets domestic issues prevail, it is in deep trouble.

Meanwhile bin Laden remains at large. And the source of the post-9/11 anthrax terror is unknown—an even more striking failure, given that the source is assumed to be domestic, perhaps even from a federal weapons lab. The Iraqi weapons of mass destruction have been quietly forgotten.

For the second 9/11 anniversary and beyond, we basically have two choices. We can march forward with confidence that the global enforcer will drive evil from the world, much as the president's speechwriters declare, plagiarizing ancient epics and children's tales.

Or we can subject the doctrines of the proclaimed grand new era to scrutiny, drawing rational conclusions, perhaps gaining some sense of the emerging reality.

The wars that are contemplated in the "war on terror" are to go on for a long time. "There's no telling how many wars it will take to secure freedom in the homeland," the president announced last year (2002). That's fair enough. Potential and concocted threats are limitless. And there is strong reason to believe that real threats are becoming more severe as a result of Bush administration lawlessness and violence.

We should also be able to appreciate recent comments on the matter by the 1996–2000 head of Israel's General Security Service (Shabak, Shin Bet), Ami Ayalon, who observed that "those who want victory" against terror without addressing underlying grievances "want an unending war."

The observation generalizes in obvious ways.

The world has good reason to watch what is happening in Washington with fear and trepidation. It cannot be stressed too often that the people who are best placed to relieve those fears are the people of the United States, who are fortunate in that they can do more than anyone else to shape the future, thanks to the power of their own state and the freedom and privilege they enjoy, very high by comparative standards.

NOTES

1. The Taliban requested evidence to support the U.S. demand that they turn over Osama bin Laden and associates. The Bush administration refused to provide any—because, we later learned, they did not have any. Eight months later, the head of the FBI, Robert Mueller, informed the press that the FBI by then "believed" that the 9/11 plot was hatched in Afghanistan but was implemented in the United Arab Emirates and Europe. Three weeks after the bombing was initiated, the official goals were shifted: British Admiral Sir Michael Boyce informed Afghans that they would be bombed "until they get the leadership changed," a textbook example of extreme state terrorism. The bombing was bitterly denounced by leading Afghan opponents of the

Taliban, including U.S. favorite Abdul Haq, who pleaded with Washington to stop killing innocent Afghans just to "show off its muscle," meanwhile undermining their efforts to overthrow the Taliban from within; realistically, it appears in retrospect. The bombing was also strongly opposed in most of the world, the international Gallup Poll revealed, vigorously so if civilians were targeted, as they were from the start. The poll was apparently not reported in the United States. The bombing was undertaken with the expectation that it might drive several million people over the edge of starvation, and for that reason was harshly denounced by virtually all international aid agencies. Months later, Harvard's leading specialist on Afghanistan, Samina Ahmed, wrote in the Harvard journal *International Security* (Winter 2001-2) that "[b]ecause humanitarian assistance was disrupted by U.S. military strikes, millions of Afghans are at grave risk of starvation." It is a remarkable commentary on Western moral and intellectual culture that this operation is presented as a textbook example of "just war," no questions raised.

The United States and the United Nations

OCTOBER 17, 2003

Faced with the remarkable failures of the military occupation of Iraq, the United States asked the United Nations to shoulder some of the costs.

The UN Security Council passed the U.S.-British resolution (Resolution 1511) unanimously but not unequivocally. China, France, and Russia, permanent members of the Security Council, opposed the resolution and will not offer troops or more money but, along with Germany, Pakistan, and others, submitted to U.S. pressure to preserve symbolic unity.

Serious divisions remain, especially regarding if and when the occupiers will transfer meaningful political power to the Iraqis.

The mixed response to the resolution reflects a history of Washington high-handedness toward the international community and the United Nations itself.

The U.S.-led war in Iraq went forward without UN backing. Washington acted in line with the National Security Strategy that the Bush administration announced last year in September (2002), which asserted the U.S. right to use force, unilaterally if necessary, against a perceived enemy.

Consistently, when the United Nations fails to serve as a U.S. instrument, Washington dismisses it. Last year (2002), for example, the UN Committee on Disarmament and International Security adopted a resolution that called for stronger measures to prevent the militarization of space, and another that reaffirmed the 1925 Geneva Protocol against the use of poisonous gases and bacteriological warfare. Both resolutions passed unanimously, with two abstentions: the United States and Israel. In practice, U.S. abstention amounts to a veto.

Since the 1960s the United States has been far in the lead in vetoing UN Security Council resolutions, even those calling on states to observe international law. Britain is second; France and Russia far behind. Even that record is skewed by the fact that Washington's enormous power often compels the weakening of resolutions to which it objects, or keeps crucial matters off the agenda entirely.

The routine use of the veto by the world champion is generally ignored or downplayed in the United States or sometimes hailed as a principled stand of embattled Washington. But this stance is not interpreted as eroding the legitimacy and credibility of the United Nations, as it clearly does. Rather, the unwillingness of others to follow the U.S. lead is seen as the problem—a display of arrogance that wins few friends.

Throughout the UN debate on Iraq, Washington has insisted on its prerogative to act unilaterally. At a news conference on March 6 (2003), for example, Bush stated that there is only "a single question: Has the Iraqi regime fully and unconditionally disarmed as required by [UN Resolution] 1441, or has it not?" He left no doubt that the decision is for the U.S. to make, not anyone else, certainly not the UN. Furthermore, he went on immediately to make it clear that the answer did not matter, announcing that "when it comes to our security we really don't need anyone's permission."

UN inspections and Security Council deliberations were therefore a farce, and even completely verified compliance would be irrelevant. The United States would institute the regime of its choice in Iraq even if Saddam had disarmed completely; in fact, even if Saddam and his family had left the country, as the president said at the Azores Summit on the eve of the invasion.

When the occupying army failed to discover Iraqi weapons of mass destruction, the administration shifted its stance from "absolute certainty" about the existence of the weapons and argued that the United States is entitled to act against any nation that has even the intent to develop weapons of mass destruction. Lowering the bar for the resort to force is the most significant consequence of the collapse of the proclaimed rationale for the invasion.

Today the paramount issue still is who rules Iraq. Few trust the United States to establish a government that will be permitted to be independent. Therefore world opinion is strongly in favor of the United Nations taking over, as is U.S. public opinion, according to polls since April (2003) by the Program on International Policy Attitudes (PIPA) at the University of Maryland.

Iraqi opinion is hard to judge, but a recent (2003) Gallup Poll in Baghdad shows that the foreign figure with the most favorable rating was Chirac, far above Bush or Blair. French President Chirac was, of course, the most prominent international critic of the invasion.

Through all the shifts of justifications and pretexts, one principle remains invariant: The United States must end up in effective control of Iraq, under some facade of democracy if that proves feasible.

The basic lines of U.S. thinking were illustrated in the organization chart of the "Civil Administration of Postwar Iraq." There are sixteen boxes, each containing a name in boldface and a designation of the person's responsibility, from Presidential Envoy Paul Bremer at the top (answering to the Pentagon), down through the chart. Seven are generals; most of the rest are U.S. government officials. At the very bottom, there is a seventeenth box, about one-third the size of the others, with no names, no boldface and no functions: It reads, "Iraqi ministry advisers."

President Bush has sought to share the costs but not power in postwar Iraq. Washington must be in charge, not the United Nations, not the Iraqi people.

Dilemmas of Dominance

NOVEMBER 26, 2003

As the United States struggles to impose order on Iraq, along with a regime that will be subordinated to U.S. interests, another crisis threatens to erupt in North Korea.

In the so-called axis of evil, North Korea is the most dangerous member. But like Iran (and unlike Iraq) it failed the first of the U.S. criteria for a legitimate target: It was not defenseless.

North Korea has a deterrent—not nuclear weapons (at the time of writing), but massed artillery at the Demilitarized Zone, aimed at Seoul, the capital of South Korea, and at tens of thousands of American troops just south of the border. The troops are scheduled to be withdrawn, outside of artillery range, arousing concerns in North and South Korea about U.S. intentions.

In October 2002, the United States charged that North Korea had secretly begun a program to enrich uranium, in violation of a 1994 agreement. The nuclear brinkmanship since then has reminded some observers of the Cuban Missile Crisis. This year (2003), Washington has taught an ugly lesson to the world: If you want to defend yourself from us, you had better mimic North Korea and pose a credible military threat.[1]

North Korea also failed a second criterion for a U.S. target: It is one of the poorest and most miserable countries in the world.

But North Korea has a geostrategic significance that might make it subject to U.S. attack—if the deterrent can be countered. North Korea lies within Northeast Asia, a region that presents its own challenge to Washington's dreams of global dominance.

Three global economic centers are facing off: the United States, Europe and Northeast Asia, in a new form of the "tripolar" world system that has been emerging for thirty years.

In one dimension, the military dimension, the United States is in a class by itself, but not in others. The regions are maneuvering in a competition for power despite complex linkages among them and substantially shared elite interests.

A recent study by the Task Force on U.S. Korea Policy—directed by Selig S. Harrison for the Center for International Policy in Washington, and the Center for East Asian Studies in Chicago—examines the issues arising for Northeast Asia and for the world.

Northeast Asia is now the world's most dynamic economic region, with close to 30 percent of global gross domestic product, far more than the United States (19 percent), and half of global foreign exchange reserves. The United States and Europe now trade more with Northeast Asia than with one another.

Northeast Asia encompasses two major industrial societies, Japan and South Korea, and China is becoming an industrial society. Siberia is rich in natural resources, including oil. The region is increasing its internal trade and connecting to the Southeast Asian countries in an informal association sometimes called ASEAN plus three: China, Japan and South Korea.

Pipelines are being built from the resource centers, like Siberia, to the industrial centers. Some of those pipelines would naturally go through North Korea to South Korea, and the Trans-Siberian Railway could be extended on the same course.

The United States is ambivalent about this Northeast Asian integration. Washington's concern is that integrated regions like Europe or Northeast Asia might seek a more independent course and become what used to be called a "third force" during the Cold War years.

The Task Force on U.S. Korea Policy recommends that Washington seek a diplomatic solution to the current crisis over North Korea, a process begun haltingly and unevenly under Clinton, "guaranteeing the security of a non-nuclear North Korea, promoting the reconciliation of North and South Korea, and drawing North Korea into economic engagement with its neighbors." Such interactions could accelerate economic reforms in North Korea, leading in time "to a diffusion of economic power that would loosen totalitarian political controls and moderate human rights abuses."

These policies would conform to the regional consensus. The alternative—confrontation in the manner of the Bush-Cheney-Rumsfeld grand strategy of preventive war—"could drag Northeast Asia and the United States into an unwanted war," the Task Force argues.

A more temperate policy might encourage Northeast Asia, like Europe, to follow a more independent course, which, however, would make it harder for the United States to maintain a global order in which others must respect their proper place.

Energy dependence has had a central place in these interactions. Since World War II, U.S. planners have sought to control the incomparable Middle East energy resources as, effectively, a lever of world control. Recognizing the same basic facts of life, Europe and rising Asian powers have sought to obtain their own resources free from what the prominent planner George Kennan called the "veto power" of U.S. control of energy supplies and sea lanes. Much of the conflict over the Middle East, as well as Central Asia, reflects these concerns.

The United States has long reacted harshly to the "successful defiance" of Third World countries like Cuba that sought a path to independent development, assigning priority to domestic needs rather than those of foreign investors and Washington planners. For Washington, the concerns have always reached the industrial heartlands of the major powers as well—now more than ever as the basically "tripolar" character of the world economic order takes new forms.

The invasion of Iraq was an "exemplary action," demonstrating to the world that the Bush administration meant quite seriously its doctrine of using force at will to assert its global dominance and to bar any potential challenge, however remote. Others surely attend to the lesson.

Violence is a powerful instrument of control, as history demonstrates. But the dilemmas of dominance are not slight.

NOTES

1. By 2006, North Korea had developed an estimated eight to ten nuclear weapons, had resumed long-range missile tests, and had conducted a nuclear test, apparently a failure. These developments can be added to the record of Bush's achievements. "When President Bush took office," Leon Sigal writes in the November 2006 issue of *Current History*, "the North Koreans had stopped testing longer-range missiles. It had one or two bombs' worth of plutonium and was verifiably not making more." Sigal, one of the leading specialists on the topic, reviews the record and concludes that North Korea "has been playing tit for tat—reciprocating whenever Washington cooperates and retaliating whenever Washington reneges—in an effort to end enmity." In one important case, in 1993 North Korea was about to strike a deal with Israel to end missile exports to the Middle East in

return for diplomatic recognition, a deal that would have greatly enhanced Israeli security. But the United States "leaned on Israel to call off the missile deal," as it did; in the relation of dependency it has chosen, Israel must follow orders. North Korea retaliated by carrying out its first test of a medium-range missile. The pattern continued through the Clinton years. Bush's aggressive militarism had the pre-dictable effects, just as it had (as predicted) provoked development of offensive military weaponry by Russia and later China. After Bush's 2002 charges, North Korea returned to development of missiles and nuclear weapons. Eventually, under pressure from Asian countries, the Bush administration agreed to negotiations, leading to an agree-ment in September 2005 that North Korea would abandon "all nuclear weapons and existing weapons programs" and allow international inspections, in return for international aid and a non-aggression pledge from the U.S., with an agreement that the two sides would "respect each other's sovereignty, exist peacefully together and take steps to nor-malize relations." The Bush administration immediately undermined the accord, disbanding the international con-sortium set up to provide the promised light-water reactor, renewing the threat of force, and pressuring banks to freeze North Korea's hard currency accounts, including proceeds from legitimate foreign trade. (See Sigal; *Financial Times*, October 10, 2006; Professor Thomas Kim, Executive Direc-tor of the Korea Policy Institute, www.kpolicy.org.)

Washington claimed that North Korea was using the banks for counterfeiting U.S. currency. The credibility of Bush administration claims is so low that one cannot draw any conclusions from the allegation. The conservative *Frankfurter Allgemeine Zeitung* reports that the counterfeiting may be a CIA operation ("Geldfälschung: Stammen die 'Supernotes' von der CIA?," January 6, 2007).

By February 2007, "increasing pressure on the North Korean regime and an embattled US administration seeking success in its dealings with one of the 'axes of evil' have helped breathe life into a process long considered terminal" (Anna Fifield, "Negotiators seek right chemistry to curb N Korea's nuclear ambitions," *Financial Times*, February 8, 2007). More accurately, an "embattled US administration" grasping for some straw of success agreed to return to negotiations. The preferred version in the U.S. was that the dogged U.S. negotiator Christopher Hill, the main source quoted, is "trying to return the process to September 2005," when "talks on carrying out the provisions broke down" for reasons left obscure, "and North Korea then defied international warnings by testing a nuclear device" (Jim Yardley, "Nuclear Talks On North Korea Set to Resume in Beijing," *New York Times*, February 8, 2007). That's not quite the full story. An agreement was reached similar to the one that Washington had scuttled in September 2005. At the same time, Washington conceded that its 2002 charges were based on dubious evidence. The concession is thought to be "preventative," out of concern that if international arms inspectors enter North Korea under the new agreement, Washington's charges on the basis of alleged intelligence may "once again be compared to what is actually found on the ground," suffering the same fate as in Iraq (David Sanger and William Broad, "U.S. Concedes Uncertainty On Korean Uranium Effort," *New York Times*, March 1, 2007).

As Sigal observes, there are lessons from all of this: diplomacy can work, if conducted in good faith.

Saddam Hussein Before the Tribunal

DECEMBER 15, 2003

All people who have any concern for human rights, justice and integrity should be overjoyed by the capture of Saddam Hussein, and should be awaiting a fair trial for him by an international tribunal.[1]

An indictment of Saddam's atrocities would include not only his slaughter and gassing of Kurds in 1988 but also, rather crucially, his massacre of the Shiite rebels who might have overthrown him in 1991.

At the time, Washington and its allies held the "strikingly unanimous view (that) whatever the sins of the Iraqi leader, he offered the West and the region a better hope for his country's stability than did those who have suffered his repression," reported Alan Cowell in the *New York Times*. The term "stability" is a codename for subordination to U.S. interests. There was no contradiction, for example, when liberal policy analyst James Chace, former editor of *Foreign Affairs*, observed in the May 22, 1977 issue of the *New York Times Magazine* that Nixon-Kissinger "efforts to destabilize a freely elected Marxist government in Chile" were undertaken because "we were determined to seek stability."

Last December (2002), Jack Straw, Britain's foreign secretary, released a dossier of Saddam's crimes drawn almost entirely from the period of firm U.S.-British support of Saddam. With the usual display of moral integrity, Straw's report and Washington's reaction overlooked that support.

Such practices often employ a device deeply rooted in the intellectual culture, the doctrine of "change of course," invoked in the United States every two or three years. The content of the doctrine is, "Yes, in the past we did some wrong things because of innocence or inadvertence. But now that's all over, so let's not waste any more time on this boring, stale stuff."

The doctrine is dishonest and cowardly but it does have advantages: It protects us from the danger of understanding what is happening before our eyes.

For example, the Bush administration's original proclaimed reason for going to war in Iraq was to save the world from a tyrant developing weapons of mass destruction and cultivating links to terror. Nobody believes that now, not even Bush's speechwriters.

After the earlier claims collapsed, a new reason for the war took center stage: we invaded Iraq to establish a democracy there and, in fact, to democratize the whole Middle East.

Sometimes the repetition of this democracy-building posture reaches the level of rapturous acclaim. Last month (November 2003), for example, David Ignatius, the *Washington Post* commentator, described the invasion of Iraq as "the most idealistic war in modern times"—fought solely to bring democracy to Iraq and the region.

Ignatius was particularly impressed with Paul Wolfowitz, "the Bush administration's idealist in chief," whom he describes as a genuine intellectual who "bleeds for [the Arab world's] oppression and dreams of liberating it."

Maybe that helps explain Wolfowitz's career—like his strong support for Suharto in Indonesia, one of the twentieth century's worst mass murderers and aggressors, when Wolfowitz was ambassador to that country under President Reagan and was one of Suharto's strongest supporters, in later years as well.[2]

As the State Department official responsible for East Asian Pacific affairs under Reagan, Wolfowitz oversaw support for the murderous dictators Chun of South Korea and Marcos of the Philippines.

All this is irrelevant because of the convenient doctrine of change of course. So, yes, Wolfowitz's heart bleeds for the victims of oppression—and if the record shows the opposite, it's just that boring old stuff that we want to forget about.

One might recall another recent illustration of Wolfowitz's love of democracy. The Turkish Parliament, heeding its population's near-unanimous opposition to war in Iraq, refused to let U.S. forces deploy fully from Turkey. This caused absolute fury in Washington.

Wolfowitz took the most extreme position. He denounced the Turkish military for failing to intervene to overturn the decision and demanded that they apologize to the U.S. for this misdeed. Turkey was listening to its people, not taking orders from Crawford, Texas.

The most recent chapter is Wolfowitz's "Determination and Findings" on bidding for lavish reconstruction contracts in Iraq. Excluded are countries where the government dared to take the same position as the vast majority of the population. Wolfowitz's alleged grounds are "security interests," which are nonexistent, though the visceral hatred of democracy is hard to miss—along with the fact that Halliburton and Bechtel will now be free to "compete" with the vibrant democracies of Uzbekistan and the Solomon Islands, but not with leading industrial societies.

What's revealing and important for the future is that Washington's display of contempt for democracy went side by side with a chorus of adulation about its yearning for democracy. To be able to carry that off is an impressive achievement, hard to mimic even in a totalitarian state.

Iraqis have some insight into this process of conquerors and conquered.

The British created Iraq for their own interests. When they ran that part of the world, they discussed how to set up what they called Arab facades—weak, pliable governments, parliamentary if possible, so long as the British effectively ruled.

Who would expect that the United States would ever intend to permit an independent Iraqi government to exist? Especially now that Washington has reserved the right to set up permanent military bases there, in the heart of the world's greatest oil-producing region, and has imposed an economic regime that no sovereign country would accept, putting the country's fate in the hands of Western corporations.

Throughout history, even the harshest and most shameful measures are regularly accompanied by professions of noble intent—and rhetoric about bestowing freedom and independence.

An honest look would only generalize Thomas Jefferson's observation on the world situation of his day: "We believe no more in Bonaparte's fighting merely for the liberties of the seas, than in Great Britain's fighting for the liberties of mankind. The object is the same, to draw to themselves the power, the wealth and the resources of other nations."

NOTES

1. Saddam Hussein was tried and executed for his role in the murder of some 150 people in 1982, a triviality by his horrendous standards. The trial was condemned as seriously unfair by the major human rights organizations. Commentary entirely ignored the significance of 1982 in U.S.-Iraqi affairs. On that matter, see page 142.

If U.S.-U.K. support for Saddam was mentioned at all, which was rare, it was excused on the grounds that Iraq was fighting Iran, a more dangerous enemy. The pretext is without merit. Both the U.S. and U.K. continued their support for Saddam without notable change, including provision of means to develop weapons of mass destruction, after the end of the war with Iran. In 1989, Iraqi nuclear engineers were invited to the U.S. for advanced training. In April 1990, four months before Saddam's invasion of Kuwait, a high-level senatorial delegation, led by 1996 Republican presidential candidate Bob Dole, went to Iraq to convey President Bush's good wishes to Saddam and to assure him that he need not be concerned with the criticisms he hears from some maverick commentators in the United States. Support continued until the Kuwait invasion. The British record was worse.

2. Wolfowitz's appointment as president of the World Bank in 2005 was accompanied by laudatory articles on his dedication to democracy and development, and his struggle against corruption. Ignored was his atrocious record in undermining human rights and democracy in Indonesia, which was bitterly condemned by activists there at the same time, his role in the collapse of the economy, and the report by Transparency International at the same time that his friend Suharto was by far the world champion for corruption. For details, see *Failed States*, page 133 and what follows.

Saddam Hussein and Crimes of State

JANUARY 22, 2004

The long, tortuous association between Saddam Hussein and the West raises questions about what issues—and embarrassments—may surface at a tribunal.[1]

In a (virtually unimaginable) fair trial for Saddam, a defense attorney could quite rightly call to the stand Colin Powell, Dick Cheney, Donald Rumsfeld, Bush I, and other high officials of the Reagan-Bush administrations who provided significant support for the dictator even through his worst atrocities.

A fair trial would at least accept the elementary moral principle of universality: The accusers and the accused must be subject to the same standards. In war crimes tribunals the precedents are murky. Even at Nuremberg, the least defective of such tribunals (and with the worst collection of gangsters likely ever to be assembled), the operational definition of "crime" was something the Germans did and the Allies didn't.

"Hussein, like Milosevic, will try to embarrass the West by talking about its past support for his regime—legally irrelevant, but something to make both Jacques Chirac and Donald Rumsfeld wince," Gary J. Bass, a professor at Princeton University and author of *Stay the Hand of Vengeance: The Politics of War Crimes Tribunals* (2000), recently wrote in the *Boston Globe*.

For a truly fair trial, it's surely relevant, as an abundance of congressional and other records show, that Washington made an unholy accommodation with Saddam during the 1980s. The initial pretext was that Iraq staved off Iran—which it attacked with U.S. backing—but the same support continued well after the war was over.

Now those responsible for the policies of accommodation are bringing Saddam to the bar of justice.

Rumsfeld, as Reagan's special envoy to the Middle East, visited Iraq in 1983 and 1984 to establish firmer relations with Saddam (at the same time that the administration was criticizing Iraq for using chemical weapons).

Powell was Bush I's national security adviser from December 1987 to January 1989, and a few months later became chairman of the Joint Chiefs of Staff. Cheney was Bush I's defense secretary. Thus Powell and Cheney were in top decision-making positions for the period of Saddam's worst atrocities, the massacre and gassing of the Kurds in 1988 and the crushing of the Shiite rebellion in 1991 that might have overthrown him.

Today, under Bush II, Powell, Cheney, and others constantly bring up those atrocities to justify beating the devil—rightly, though the crucial element of U.S. support of Saddam during this period is missing.

In October 1989, Bush I issued a national security directive, declaring that "normal relations between the United States and Iraq would serve our longer-term interests and promote stability in both the Gulf and the Middle East."

The United States offered subsidized food supplies that Saddam's regime badly needed after its destruction of Kurdish agricultural production, along with advanced technology and biological agents adaptable to weapons of mass destruction.

After Saddam stepped out of line and invaded Kuwait in August 1990, politics and pretexts varied, but one element remained constant: the people of Iraq must not control their country.

In 1990 the United Nations imposed economic sanctions on Iraq, administered mainly by the United States and Britain. These sanctions, which continued through President Clinton and into Bush II, are perhaps the sorriest legacy of U.S. policy toward Iraq.

No Westerners know Iraq better than Denis Halliday and Hans von Sponeck, who served successively as UN humanitarian coordinators there from 1997 to 2000. Both resigned in protest of the sanctions regime, which Halliday has characterized as "genocidal." As Halliday, von Sponeck, and others had pointed out for years, the sanctions devastated the Iraqi population while strengthening Saddam and his clique, increasing the people's dependency on the tyrant for their survival.

"We have sustained [the Saddam regime] and denied the opportunities for change," Halliday said in 2002. "I believe if the Iraqis had their economy, had their lives back, and had their way of life restored, they would take care of the form of governance that they want, that they believe is suitable to their country."[2]

Whether or not this history is permitted to come out in a tribunal, the issue of who will be in charge in Iraq in the future still remains crucial and is highly contested right at this moment.

Apart from that crucial issue, those who have been concerned with the tragedy of Iraq had three basic goals: (1) overthrowing the tyranny, (2) ending the sanctions that were targeting the people, not the rulers, and (3) preserving some semblance of world order.

There can be no disagreement among decent people on the first two goals: achieving them is an occasion for rejoicing, particularly for those who protested U.S. support for Saddam and later opposed the murderous sanctions regime. They can therefore applaud without hypocrisy.

The second goal could surely have been achieved, and possibly the first as well, without undermining the third.

The Bush administration has openly declared its intention to dismantle much of what remained of the system of world order and to rule the world by force, with Iraq as a demonstration project.

That intention has elicited fear and often hatred throughout the world, and despair among those who are concerned about the likely consequences of choosing to remain complicit with the current policies of U.S. aggression at will. That is, of course, a choice very largely in the hands of the American people.

NOTES

1. As mentioned earlier, the tribunal was restricted to crimes of 1982, very slight by Saddam's standards, hence ensuring that the disgraceful role of the U.S., Britain, and others in supporting his crimes did not surface—or even the significance of 1982 in U.S.-Iraqi relations.

2. On the horrifying impact of the sanctions, and the primary U.S.-U.K. role in ensuring savage punishment of the population of Iraq, see Hans von Sponeck's *A Different Kind of War: The UN Sanctions Regime in Iraq* (2006). Von Sponeck resigned as director of the Oil-for-Food program in 2000, regarding it as in violation of the Genocide Convention. As noted, his predecessor Denis Halliday, also a distinguished international diplomat, had resigned on the same grounds. The Clinton administration blocked their efforts to inform the Security Council of the true situation. As explained by

State Department spokesperson James Rubin, "this man in Baghdad is paid to work, not to speak." The U.S. media adopted the same position. Halliday and von Sponeck knew more about Iraq than any Westerner. However—or maybe therefore—their voices were not to be heard in the U.S. mainstream during the years leading to the invasion.

A Wall as a Weapon

FEBRUARY 23, 2004

It is a virtual reflex for governments to plead security concerns when they undertake any controversial action, often as a pretext for something else. Careful scrutiny is always in order. Israel's so-called security fence, which is the subject of hearings starting today at the International Court of Justice in The Hague, is a case in point.[1]

Few would question Israel's right to protect its citizens from terrorist attacks like the one yesterday, even to build a security wall if that were an appropriate means. It is also clear where such a wall would be built if security were the guiding concern: inside Israel, within the internationally recognized border, the Green Line established after the 1948–49 war. The wall could then be as forbidding as the authorities chose: patrolled by the army on both sides, heavily mined, impenetrable. Such a wall would maximize security, and there would be no international protest or violation of international law.

This observation is well understood. While Britain supports America's opposition to the Hague hearings, its foreign minister, Jack Straw, has written that the wall is "unlawful." Another ministry official, who inspected the "security fence," said it should be on the Green Line or "indeed on the Israeli side of the line." A British parliamentary investigative commission also called for the wall to be built on Israeli land, condemning the barrier as part of a "deliberate" Israeli "strategy of bringing the population to heel."

What this wall is really doing is taking Palestinian lands. It is also—as the Israeli sociologist Baruch Kimmerling has described Israel's war of "politicide" against the Palestinians—helping turn Palestinian communities into dungeons, next to which the Bantustans of South Africa look like symbols of freedom, sovereignty and self-determination.

Even before construction of the barrier was under way, the United Nations estimated that Israeli barriers, infrastructure projects, and settlements had created fifty largely disconnected Palestinian pockets in the West Bank. As the design of the wall was coming into view, the World Bank estimated that it might isolate 250,000 to 300,000 Palestinians, more than 10 percent of the population, and that it might effectively annex up to 10 percent of West Bank land. And when the government of Ariel Sharon finally published its proposed map, it became clear the wall would cut the West Bank into sixteen isolated enclaves, confined to just 42 percent of the West Bank land that Mr. Sharon had previously said could be ceded to a Palestinian state, according to an analysis of UN reports by Harvard University Middle East scholar Sara Roy.

The wall has already claimed some of the most fertile lands of the West Bank. And, crucially, it extends Israel's control of critical water resources, which Israel and its settlers can appropriate as they choose, while the indigenous population often lacks water for drinking.

Palestinians in the "seam" between the wall and the Green Line will be permitted to apply for the right to live in their own homes; Israelis automatically have the right to use these lands. "Hiding behind security rationales and the seemingly neutral bureaucratic language of military orders is the gateway for expulsion," the Israeli journalist Amira Hass wrote in the daily *Haaretz*. "Drop by drop, unseen, not so many that it would be noticed internationally and shock public opinion." The same is true of the regular killings, terror, and daily brutality and humiliation of the past thirty-five years of harsh occupation, while land and resources have been taken for settlers enticed by ample subsidies, thanks to the gracious paymaster abroad, though not with the support of the American population.[2]

It also seems likely that Israel will transfer to the occupied West Bank the 7,500 settlers it said this month (February 2004) it would remove from the Gaza Strip. These Israelis now enjoy ample land and fresh water, while one million Palestinians barely survive, their meager water supplies virtually unusable. Gaza is a cage, and as the city of Rafah in the south is systematically demolished, residents may be blocked from any contact with Egypt while also blockaded from the sea.

It is misleading to call these Israeli policies. They are U.S.-Israeli policies—made possible by unremitting United States military, economic, diplomatic, and not least ideological support: namely, the way the events are generally portrayed in media and the intellectual culture.

This has been particularly true since 1971 when, with Washington's support, Israel rejected a full peace offer from Egypt, preferring expansion to security. In 1976, the United States vetoed a Security Council resolution calling for a two-state settlement in accord with an overwhelming international consensus. The two-state proposal has the support of a majority of Americans today and could be enacted immediately if Washington wanted to do so.

At most, the Hague hearings will end in an advisory ruling that the wall is illegal. It will change nothing. Any real chance for a political settlement—and for decent lives for the people of the region—depends on the United States.

NOTES

1. On the brutal impact of Israel's wall on the Palestinian population, see among many other studies, *Under the Guise of Security: Routing the Separation Barrier to Enable the Expansion of Israeli Settlements in the West Bank* (B'Tselem, December 2005). All of this occurs in brazen violation of international law and the World Court, but proceeds essentially unhampered thanks to U.S. support, under President Bush with his official endorsement, instead of merely his tacit endorsement as before. See also Sara Roy, "The Palestinian State: Division and Despair," *Current History*, January 2004.

2. A large majority of the U.S. population feels that aid should be eliminated for either of the two partners, Israel and Palestinians, which refuses to engage in good faith negotiations for a political settlement in terms of the international consensus. That means cutting off aid to Israel, though probably few are aware of the fact. The polls receive scarce if any mention, and the matter is not discussed. For more on this see *Hegemony or Survival*, pages 168-9.

The United States: Terrorist Sanctuary

MARCH 5, 2004

Every self-respecting president has a doctrine attached to his name. The core principle of the Bush II doctrine is that the United States must "rid the world of evil," as the president said right after 9/11.

A special responsibility is to wage war against terrorism, with the corollary that any state that harbors terrorists is a terrorist state and should be treated accordingly.

Let's ask a fair and simple question: What would the consequences be if we were to take the Bush doctrine seriously and treat states that harbor terrorists as terrorist states, subject to bombardment and invasion?

The United States has long been a sanctuary to a rogues' gallery of people whose actions qualify them as terrorists and whose presence undermines U.S. proclaimed principles.

In this connection, consider the case of the Cuban Five, Cuban nationals convicted in Miami in 2001 as part of a spy ring. The Cuban Five appeal is scheduled for March 10 (2004) in Miami.[1]

To understand the case, which has prompted international protests, we have to look at the sordid history of U.S.-Cuba relations (leaving aside here the issue of the crushing, decades-long U.S. embargo in violation of General Assembly Resolutions in which the U.S. is virtually isolated).

The United States has engaged in large- and small-scale terrorist attacks against Cuba since 1959, including the Bay of Pigs invasion, the bizarre plots to kill Castro, and far more serious terrorist attacks in Cuba and against Cubans abroad. In the Kennedy years, the operations were directed by Robert Kennedy, whose highest priority was to bring "the terrors of the earth" to Cuba, according to his biographer, historian and Kennedy-adviser Arthur Schlesinger. The terrorist operations were resumed by Kennedy after the missile crisis, cancelled by Lyndon Johnson, resumed again under Nixon.

The government's direct participation in the attacks ended during the late 1970s—at least officially.

In 1989, Bush I granted a pardon to Orlando Bosch, one of the most notorious anti-Castro terrorists, accused of masterminding the bombing of a Cuban airliner in 1976 which killed seventy-three people. Bush overruled the Justice Department, which had refused an asylum request from Bosch, concluding, "The security of this nation is affected by its ability to urge credibly other nations to refuse aid and shelter to terrorists, whose target we too often become."

Recognizing that the United States was going to harbor anti-Castro terrorists, Cuban agents infiltrated those networks. In 1998, high-level FBI officials were sent to Havana, where they were given thousands of pages of documentation and hundreds of hours of videotape about terrorist actions organized by cells in Florida.

The FBI reacted by arresting the people who provided the information, including a group now known as the Cuban Five.

The arrests were followed by what amounted to a show trial in Miami. The Five were convicted, three to life sentences (for espionage; and the leader, Gerardo Hernández, also for conspiracy to murder).

Meanwhile, people regarded by the FBI and Justice Department as dangerous terrorists live happily in the United States and continue to plot and implement crimes.[2]

The list of terrorists-in-residence in the United States also includes Emmanuel Constant from Haiti, known as Toto, a former paramilitary leader from the Duvalier era. Constant is the founder of the FRAPH (Front for Advancement of Progress in Haiti), the paramilitary group that carried out most of the state terror in the early 1990s under the military junta that overthrew President Aristide. At last report, Constant was living in Queens, New York.

The United States has refused Haiti's request for extradition. The reason, it is generally assumed, is that Constant might reveal ties between Washington and the military junta that killed 4,000 to 5,000 Haitians, with Constant's paramilitary forces playing the leading role.

The gangsters leading the current coup in Haiti include FRAPH leaders.

For the United States, Cuba has long been the primary concern in the hemisphere. A declassified 1964 State Department document declares Fidel Castro to be an intolerable threat because he "represents a successful defiance of the United States, a negation of our whole hemispheric policy of almost a century and a half," since the Monroe Doctrine declared that no challenge to U.S. dominance would be tolerated in the hemisphere.

Venezuela now presents a similar problem of successful defiance. A recent lead article in the *Wall Street Journal* says, "Fidel Castro has found a key benefactor and heir apparent to the cause of derailing the U.S.'s agenda in Latin America: Venezuelan President Hugo Chavez."

Last month (February 2004), Venezuela asked the United

States to extradite two former military officers who are seeking asylum in the United States. The two had taken part in a military coup, which, before its overthrow by a popular uprising, had disbanded the parliament, the Supreme Court, and all other vestiges of democracy—all with the support of Washington, endlessly lauded for its dedication to "democracy promotion," though criticized as perhaps excessive in its zeal.

The Venezuelan government, remarkably, observed a ruling of the Venezuelan Supreme Court barring prosecution of the coup leaders. The two officers were later implicated in a terrorist bombing and fled to Miami.

Outrage over defiance is deeply ingrained in U.S. history. Thomas Jefferson bitterly condemned France for its "attitude of defiance" in holding New Orleans, which he coveted. Jefferson warned that France's "character [is] placed in a point of eternal friction with our character, which though loving peace and the pursuit of wealth, is high-minded."

France's "defiance [requires us to] marry ourselves to the British fleet and nation," Jefferson advised, reversing his earlier attitudes, which reflected France's crucial contribution to the liberation of the colonies from British rule.

Thanks to Haiti's liberation struggle, unaided and almost universally opposed, France's defiance soon ended. But, then as now, the guiding principles remain in place, determining friend and foe.

NOTES

1. After a complex legal history, the trial decision stands as of March 2007, and appeals continue.
2. One of the most notorious international terrorists, Luis Posada Carriles (Bosch's presumed accomplice in the

Cubana airline bombing, among many other crimes),
entered the U.S. illegally in 2005 and is being held on that
charge. Requests for extradition by Venezuela (for the
bombing) and Cuba (for the bombing and other crimes)
have been denied. Mexico and other countries have refused
to accept him. The Justice Department refuses to designate
him a terrorist, leaving him in the hands of the immigration
service. In February 2007, a federal judge denied his request
to be released on bail pending a decision on deportation.

Dangerous Times: The U.S.-Iraq War and Its Aftermath

MARCH 18, 2004

Whatever their source, the monstrous bombings in Madrid resonate all the more powerfully and painfully on the eve of the first anniversary of the U.S.-led invasion of Iraq, depicted as a reaction to the 9/11 terrorist attack.

During the year since the war against Iraq began, the predictions of many analysts have proven accurate, particularly the consequences of the cycle of violence-begetting-violence.

The U.S.-led war against Iraq was undertaken with the general recognition that it might well lead to proliferation of weapons of mass destruction and terror, risks that the Bush administration apparently considered insignificant compared with the prospect of gaining control over Iraq, enhancing control over the incomparable energy resources of the region, firmly establishing the norm of "preventive" war and strengthening their hold on domestic power.

In reaction to accelerated U.S. militarization from well before 9/11, Russia has sharply increased its offensive military forces, while others who see themselves as potential targets react by the means available to them: terror, for revenge or deterrence, and efforts to develop weapons of mass destruction, as in suspected programs in Iran and North Korea.

Along with Madrid, the litany of terror since 9/11 includes Baghdad, Bali, Casablanca, Istanbul, Jakarta, Jerusalem, Mombasa, Moscow and Riyadh. Sooner or later, terror and weapons of mass destruction are likely to be combined in the same hands, with awesome consequences.

Iraq's alleged links to al-Qaeda were dismissed by serious analysts, and no credible evidence has been found. But it is now beyond dispute that Iraq has, for the first time, become "a terrorist haven," as Jessica Stern, a terror specialist at Harvard, described it in a *New York Times* essay after the bombing of the UN headquarters in Baghdad last August (2003).

"Preventive war" is just a euphemism for aggression at will. It was this doctrine, not just the implementation of it in Iraq, that motivated the vast and unprecedented protests against the invasion (another worldwide protest is scheduled for March 20 [2004]). This reaction has surely raised the bars for further resort to this announced doctrine.

The David Kay investigation, along with undermining the claims concerning Iraqi weapons of mass destruction, revealed how fragile Saddam's hold on power was in the last years. It thus added additional weight to the opinion of the Westerners who knew Iraq best—UN humanitarian coordinators Denis Halliday and Hans von Sponeck—that, if the sanctions had not targeted the civilian population, Iraqis themselves might well have overthrown Saddam.

Last April (2003), as polls showed, Americans thought that the United Nations, not the United States, ought to have prime responsibility for Iraq's reconstruction, political and economic, in the postwar period.

The failure of the U.S. occupation of Iraq is surprising, given U.S. power and resources, the ending of the sanctions and the tyrant's removal, and the lack of significant outside support for resistance.

Partly because of that failure, the Bush administration has

backtracked and reached out for UN help. But the question of whether it will permit Iraq to be more than a U.S. client state remains in doubt.

Washington is constructing the world's largest diplomatic mission in Iraq, with some 3,000 personnel, as Robin Wright reported in the *Washington Post* in January (2004), a clear indication that the transfer of sovereignty is intended to be limited. That conclusion is reinforced by the U.S. insistence on the right to maintain military bases and forces in Iraq, and by the orders of U.S. proconsul Paul Bremer that the economy must be virtually opened to foreign takeover, a condition that no sovereign state would accept. Loss of control over the economy sharply reduces political sovereignty, of course, and also the prospects for healthy economic development, one of the clearest lessons of economic history.

Strong Iraqi demands for democracy and for more than nominal sovereignty have compelled the United States to back down from its efforts to impose a government that Washington can completely control, and even progress on a formal constitution does not bring that continuing conflict to an end.

In December (2003), a PIPA/Knowledge Networks poll showed that the U.S. general population offers little support for the government's efforts to maintain a powerful, permanent, military and diplomatic presence in Iraq. In the United States, popular concerns about the war and the occupation may have to do substantially with misgivings about the justice of the cause.

The tipping point may come with the U.S. presidential election. The U.S. political spectrum is pretty narrow, and people know that U.S. elections are mostly bought. John Kerry is accurately described as Bush-lite. However, sometimes, the choice between the two factions of what has been called the U.S. business party can make a difference, in this election as in 2000.

That's true for domestic as well as international affairs. The people around Bush are deeply committed to reversing the achievements of popular struggle during the past century. A short list of targets would include health care, job security and progressive taxation. The prospect of a government that serves popular interests is being dismantled.

Since the war in Iraq began, the world has become an even more precarious place. The American election represents a crossroads. In this U.S. system of immense power, small differences can translate into large outcomes, with far-reaching impact.

Iraq: The Roots of Resistance

APRIL 13, 2004

Long before the renewed outbreak of combat in Iraq, U.S. intelligence assessments recognized that Washington's "most formidable foe in Iraq in the months ahead may be the resentment of ordinary Iraqis increasingly hostile to the American military occupation," Douglas Jehl and David E. Sanger reported in the *New York Times* in September (2003). Failure to understand the roots of that hostility (not just the armed resistance that captures the headlines and TV shots) can only lead to more bloodshed and stalemate.

Even if we put aside the crucial matter of the criminal invasion, it should be clear that prolonged violent conflict, including the hideous manifestations in Fallujah and elsewhere, might not have occurred had the U.S.-led occupation been less arrogant, ignorant, and incompetent. Conquerors willing to transfer authentic sovereignty, as Iraqis demand, would have chosen a different course.

The Bush administration, among its parade of pretexts for the invasion of Iraq, has espoused a vision of a democratic revolution across the Arab world. But the most plausible reason for the invasion is conspicuously evaded: establishing secure military bases in a client state right at the heart of the world's major energy sources.

Iraqis do not evade this crucial issue. In a Gallup Poll in Baghdad, released in October (2003), asked why the United

States invaded Iraq, 1 percent of respondents said it was to establish democracy; 5 percent to help Iraqis. A plurality of the rest took Washington's motive to be to control Iraq's resources and to reorganize the Middle East in U.S. interests.

Another opinion survey in Iraq released in December (2003) by Oxford Research International is also revealing. Asked what Iraq needs right now, more than 70 percent of Iraqis chose "democracy;" 10 percent, the Coalition Provisional Authority (CPA); and 15 percent, the Iraq Interim Governing Council. By "democracy" the Iraqis meant democracy, not the nominal sovereignty that the Bush administration is designing.

In general, "people have no confidence in U.S./U.K. forces (79 percent) and the CPA (73 percent)," according to the poll. Pentagon favorite Ahmed Chalabi had no support.

The U.S.-Iraqi conflict over sovereignty was highly visible at the first anniversary of the invasion. Paul Wolfowitz and his Pentagon staff signaled "that they favor a stable, prolonged U.S. troop presence there and a relatively weak Iraqi army as the best way to nurture democracy," Stephen Glain reported in the *Boston Globe*. That is not democracy as Iraqis understand the term; or as Americans would under foreign occupation.

There would have been no point in the invasion in the first place if it did not lead to stable military bases in a dependent client state of the traditional sort. The United Nations might be brought in, but Washington is asking it to "to endorse a future Iraqi government of only nominal sovereignty and questionable legitimacy, by whose invitation the occupying powers would remain in place," the *Financial Times* commented in January (2004).

Beyond the issues of military control, Iraqis also understand the measures imposed to reduce economic sovereignty, including a series of orders to open up industries and banks to effective U.S. takeover.

Not surprisingly, the U.S. plans were condemned by Iraqi businessmen who charged that such plans would destroy domestic industry.

As for Iraqi workers, labor activist David Bacon reports that the occupying forces broke into union offices, arrested leaders, are enforcing Saddam's antilabor laws and handing over concessions to bitterly anti-union U.S. businesses.

Iraqi resentment and the failures of the military occupation have caused Washington to backtrack somewhat from the more extreme measures.

The proposals to open up the economy to effective foreign takeover excluded oil. Presumably that would have been too brazen. However, Iraqis do not have to read the *Wall Street Journal* to discover that "getting to know Iraq's ravaged oil industry in detail," thanks to lucrative contracts provided by U.S. taxpayers, "eventually could help Halliburton win mainstream energy business there," along with other state-supported multinational corporations.

It remains to be seen whether Iraqis can ever be coerced into accepting the nominal sovereignty that is offered them under the various "constitutional fictions" that are devised by the occupying power. Another question is far more important for privileged Westerners: Will they permit their governments to "nurture democracy," in the interests of the narrow sectors of power that those governments serve, over strong Iraqi opposition?

The Rules of Disengagement in Israel-Palestine

MAY 10, 2004

The Israeli-Palestinian conflict remains a prime mover of Middle East chaos and suffering. But an impasse-breaker isn't beyond reach.

In the short term, the only feasible and minimally decent solution to the conflict is along the lines of the long-standing international consensus: a two-state settlement on the internationally-recognized border (Green Line), with minor and mutual adjustments.

By now, U.S.-backed Israeli settlement and infrastructure projects change the import of "minor." Nevertheless, several two-state programs are on the table, the most prominent being the Geneva Accord, presented in December (2003) by a group of prominent Israeli and Palestinian negotiators, working outside official channels.

The Geneva Accord provides a detailed program for a 1-to-1 land swap and other aspects of a settlement, and is close to the best that is likely to be achieved in the short run—and could be achieved if the U.S. government would back it. The realpolitik is that Israel must accept what the great power dictates.

The Bush-Sharon "disengagement plan" is in fact an expansion-integration plan. Even as Sharon calls for some form of withdrawal from the Gaza Strip, "Israel will invest tens of millions of dollars in West Bank settlements," *New York Times* reporter James Bennet quotes Israeli finance minister Benjamin Netanyahu as announcing. Other reports indicate that the development will take place even on the Palestinian side of the illegal "separation wall."

Such settlements run counter to the Bush-endorsed road map, which calls for a halt to "all settlement activity."

"As important a milestone as it is, an end to Israel's occupation of the Gaza Strip requires a corresponding change in policies in the West Bank for its advantages to be realized," writes Geoffrey Aronson of the Foundation for Middle East Peace, in Washington. The Foundation has just published a map of Israeli plans for the West Bank, showing a patchwork of discontinuous, walled-off Palestinian enclaves that reproduces the worst features of South Africa's apartheid Bantustans, as Meron Benvenisti has pointed out in *Haaretz*.

The question now being raised is whether the Israeli and Palestinian communities are so intertwined in the occupied territories that no division is possible. Last November (2003), however, former leaders of Shin Bet, the Israeli General Security Service, generally agreed that Israel could and should completely pull out from the Gaza Strip. In the West Bank, 85 to 90 percent of the settlers would leave "with a simple economic plan" while there are perhaps 10 percent "with whom we will have to clash" to remove them—not a very serious problem, in the Shin Bet leaders' view.

The Geneva Accord is based on similar assumptions, which appear realistic.

It is, incidentally, quite true that none of these proposals deals with the overwhelming imbalance in military and economic power between Israel and an eventual Palestinian state, or with other quite crucial issues.

In the longer term, other arrangements might emerge, as

more healthy interactions develop between the two countries. One possibility with earlier roots is a binational federation. From 1967 to 1973, such a binational state was quite feasible in Israel-Palestine. During those years, a full peace treaty between Israel and the Arab states was also feasible and, indeed, had been offered in 1971 by Egypt, then Jordan. By 1973 the opportunity was lost.

What changed is the 1973 war and the shift in opinion among Palestinians, in the Arab world, and in the international arena in favor of Palestinian national rights, in a form that incorporated UN Security Council Resolution 242 (November 22, 1967) but added provisions for a Palestinian state in the occupied territories, which Israel would evacuate. But the United States has unilaterally blocked that resolution for the last thirty years.

The result has been wars and destruction, harsh military occupation, takeover of land and resources, resistance, and finally an increasing cycle of violence, mutual hatred, and distrust. Those outcomes cannot be wished away.

Progress requires compromises on all sides. What's a fair compromise? The closest we can come to a general formula is that compromises should be accepted if they are the best possible and can lead the way to something better.

Sharon's "two-state" settlement, leaving Palestinians caged in the Gaza Strip and in cantons in about half of the West Bank, radically fails the criterion. The Geneva Accord approximates the criterion and, therefore, should be accepted, at least as a basis for Israeli-Palestinian negotiation, in my opinion.

One of the thorniest issues is the Palestinian right of return. Palestinian refugees should certainly not be willing to renounce it, but in this world—not some imaginary world we can discuss in seminars—that right will not be exercised, in more than a limited way, within Israel. In any case it is improper to dangle hopes that will not be realized before the eyes of people suffering in misery and oppression. Rather, constructive efforts should be pursued to mitigate their suffering and deal with their problems in the real world.

A two-state settlement in accord with the international consensus is already acceptable to a very broad range of Israeli opinion. That even includes extreme hawks, who are so concerned by the "demographic problem"—the problem of too many non-Jews in a "Jewish state"—that they are even advancing the (outrageous) proposal to transfer areas of dense Arab settlement within Israel to a new Palestinian state.

A majority of the American population also supports the two-state settlement. Therefore, it is not at all inconceivable that organizing/activist efforts in the United States could bring the U.S. government into line with the international consensus, in which case, Israel would very likely go along as well.

Even without any U.S. pressure, a great many Israelis favor something of this sort—depending on exactly how questions are asked in polls. A change in Washington's position would make an enormous difference. The former leaders of Shin Bet, as well as the Israeli peace movement (Gush Shalom and others), believe that the Israeli public would accept such an outcome.

But speculation about that is not our real concern. Rather, it is to bring U.S. government policy into line with the rest of the world, and apparently with the majority of the U.S. public.

Who Is to Run the World and How?

JUNE 17, 2004

Last month (May 2004) we passed the first anniversary of President Bush's "mission accomplished" declaration of victory in Iraq.

The invasion was set in motion by the Bush doctrine, the "new imperial grand strategy," as *Foreign Affairs* called it, which declared that the United States would dominate the world for the indefinite future and destroy any challenge to that domination.

Leaving aside what is happening on the ground in Iraq, perhaps it is useful to focus on how the policies behind the invasion and occupation have made the world a much more dangerous place, the enhanced threat of terror being only one dimension.

The U.S. State Department has just admitted that its April (2004) claim that terrorism dropped—a centerpiece of the current Bush presidential campaign—was completely false. The revised report concedes that "the number of incidents and the toll in victims increased sharply."

For government planners, the most important goal was not to fight terrorism but to establish U.S. military bases in a dependent client state at the heart of the world's major energy reserves, and thus to gain an upper hand over their rivals. Zbigniew Brzezinski writes that "America's security role in the region"—in plain English, its military dominance—"gives it indirect but politically critical leverage on the European and

Asian economies that are also dependent on energy exports from the region" (*The National Interest*, Winter 2003/2004).

As Brzezinski well knows, the core problem of U.S. global dominance is that Europe and Asia (especially the dynamic Northeast Asia region) might move on an independent course. Control of the Gulf and Central Asia therefore becomes even more significant than in the past; analysts expect that the Gulf's enormous role in world energy production will continue to grow. U.S.-U.K. support for Turkmenistan, Uzbekistan, and other dictatorships in Central Asia, and the jockeying over where pipelines will go and under whose supervision, are part of the same renewed "great game."

Meanwhile, in Western commentary, it is by now ritually presupposed that the goal of the invasion was "the president's vision" of establishing democracy in Iraq.

By contrast, according to Western polls in Baghdad, this "vision"—proclaimed in Bush's "freedom agenda" in November 2003, well after the collapse of the official justifications for the invasion—is dismissed by virtually everyone, and it is generally assumed that Washington's motive for the invasion was to take control of Iraq's resources and to reorganize the Middle East in accord with U.S. interests. It is not unusual for those at the wrong end of the club to have a clearer understanding of the world in which they live.

There are plenty of other illustrations that Washington regards terrorism as a minor issue as compared to ensuring that the Middle East is under proper control. Just last month (May 2004), the Bush administration imposed economic sanctions on Syria, implementing the Syria Accountability and Lebanese Sovereignty Restoration Act passed by Congress in December 2003—virtually a declaration of war unless Syria follows U.S. commands.

Syria remains on the official U.S. list of states sponsoring terrorism, despite U.S. government acknowledgment that Syria has not sponsored terrorism for many years and that Syria has provided important intelligence to Washington on al-Qaeda and other radical Islamist groups, as Stephen Zunes writes in the spring (2004) issue of *Middle East Policy*. Thus the United States is deprived of that intelligence source in favor of achieving the higher goal—a regime that will accept U.S.-Israeli demands.

To mention just one more instance of clear but imperceptible priorities: The U.S. Treasury Department maintains an Office of Foreign Assets Control (OFAC), assigned the task of investigating suspicious financial transfers, a crucial component of the "war on terror." The agency has 120 employees. A few weeks ago (March 2004), OFAC informed Congress that, as of the end of last year (2003), four of them—only four— were dedicated to tracking the finances of Osama bin Laden and Saddam Hussein, while almost two dozen enforced the embargo against Cuba. Furthermore, OFAC reported, that the discrepancy in investigation and punishment goes back to 1990.

Why should the U.S. Treasury devote vastly more energy to strangling Cuba than to the war on terror? Successful defiance of the United States is intolerable, ranked far higher as a priority than combating terror.

To achieve domination, violence can succeed, but at tremendous cost. It can also provoke greater violence in response. Inciting terror is not the most ominous current example.

In February (2004), Russia carried out its largest military exercises in two decades, displaying new and more sophisticated weapons of mass destruction. Russian political and military leaders made clear that this arms-race revival was a

direct response to Bush administration actions and programs—especially U.S. development of low-yield nuclear
weapons, the so-called bunker busters. As strategic analysts on
both sides know, these weapons can target the bunkers, hidden
in mountains, that control Russian nuclear arsenals.

A nuclear ripple effect can follow. The Russians and Chinese
react to the United States by building up strategic weapons.
India will react to China's actions; Pakistan to India; and perhaps beyond.

Meanwhile Iraq makes its way toward what is called sovereignty. "Handover still on course," reads the headline of a
recent article by Anton La Guardia of the *London Daily Telegraph*. The last paragraph reports that "a senior British official
put it delicately: 'The Iraqi government will be fully sovereign,
but in practice it will not exercise all its sovereign functions.'"
Lord Curzon would nod sagely.

The steadfast refusal of Iraqis to accept the traditional "constitutional fictions" has compelled Washington to yield step by
step, with some assistance from the "second superpower," as
Patrick Tyler of the *New York Times* described world opinion
after the huge demonstrations of mid-February 2003, the first
time in history that mass protests against a war took place
before it had been officially launched. That makes a difference.

For example, had the recent problems in Fallujah arisen during the 1960s, they would have been resolved by B-52s and mass
murder operations on the ground.

Today, a more civilized society will not tolerate such measures as readily as in earlier years, providing at least some space
for the traditional victims to act to gain authentic independence. It is even possible that such impulses may force the Bush
administration to abandon its imperial ambitions for Iraq.

John Negroponte: From Central America to Iraq

JULY 28, 2004

One moral truism that should not provoke controversy is the principle of universality: We should apply to ourselves the same standards we apply to others—in fact, more stringent ones.

Commonly, if states have the power to do so with impunity, they disdain moral truisms, declaring themselves uniquely exempt from the principle of universality. And so we do, constantly. Every day brings new illustrations.

Just last month (June 2004), for example, John Negroponte went to Baghdad as U.S. ambassador to Iraq, heading the world's largest diplomatic mission, with the task of handing over sovereignty to Iraqis to fulfill Bush's "messianic mission" to bring democracy to the Middle East and the world, or so we are solemnly informed.

Negroponte learned his trade as U.S. ambassador to Honduras in the 1980s, during the Reaganite phase of the careers of many of the current incumbents in Washington, when the first War on Terror was underway in Central America and the Middle East.

In April (2004) Carla Anne Robbins of the *Wall Street Journal* wrote about Negroponte's Iraq appointment under the heading "Modern Proconsul." In Honduras, Negroponte was known as "'the proconsul,' a title given to powerful administrators in colonial times." There he presided over the second-largest embassy in Latin America, with the largest CIA station in the world at that time—hardly because Honduras was a centerpiece of world power.

Robbins observed that Negroponte has been criticized by human-rights activists for "covering up abuses by the Honduran military"—a euphemism for large-scale state terror—"to ensure the flow of U.S. aid" to this vital country, which was "the base for President Reagan's covert war against Nicaragua's Sandinista government." The covert war was launched after the Sandinista revolution took control in Nicaragua. Washington's professed fear was that a second Cuba might develop in this Central American nation. In Honduras, proconsul Negroponte's task was to supervise the bases where a terrorist mercenary army—the Contras—was trained, armed, and sent to overthrow the Sandinistas.

In 1984, Nicaragua responded in a way appropriate to a law-abiding state by taking its case against the United States to the World Court in The Hague. The court ordered the United States to terminate the "unlawful use of force"—in lay terms, international terrorism—against Nicaragua and to pay substantial reparations. But Washington ignored the court, then vetoed two UN Security Council resolutions affirming the judgment and calling on all states to observe international law.

U.S. State Department legal adviser Abraham D. Sofaer explained the rationale. Since most of the world cannot be "counted on to share our view," we must "reserve to ourselves the power to determine" how we will act and which matters fall "essentially within the domestic jurisdiction of the United States, as determined by the United States"—in this case the terrorist attack against Nicaragua that the court condemned.

Washington's disregard of the court decree, and its disdain

for the international community, are perhaps relevant to the current situation in Iraq.

The terrorist war in Nicaragua left a dependent and corrupt formal democracy, at an incalculable cost. Civilian deaths have been estimated at tens of thousands—proportionately, a death toll "significantly higher than the number of U.S. persons killed in the U.S. Civil War and all the wars of the twentieth century combined," writes Thomas Carothers, a leading historian of "democracy promotion" in Latin America.

Carothers writes from the perspective of an insider as well as a scholar, having served in Reagan's State Department during the "democracy enhancement" programs in Central America. The Reagan-era programs were "sincere," he believes, though a "failure," because Washington would tolerate only "limited, top-down forms of democratic change that did not risk upsetting the traditional structures of power with which the United States has long been allied."

This is a familiar historical refrain in the pursuit of visions of democracy, which Iraqis apparently comprehend, even if we choose not to.

Today, Nicaragua is the second-poorest country in the hemisphere (above Haiti, the main target of U.S. intervention during the twentieth century, Nicaragua ranking second). About 60 percent of Nicaraguan children under age two are afflicted with anemia from severe malnutrition—only one grim indication of what is hailed as a victory for freedom.

The Bush administration claims to want to bring democracy to Iraq, using the same experienced official as in Central America.

During Negroponte's confirmation hearings, the international terrorist campaign in Nicaragua received passing mention but is considered of no particular significance, thanks, presumably, to the exemption of our glorious selves from the principle of universality.

Several days after Negroponte's appointment, Honduras withdrew its small contingent of forces from Iraq. That might have been a coincidence. Or maybe the Hondurans remember something from the time when Negroponte was there that we prefer to forget.

NOTES

In February 2005, the president appointed Negroponte to be the first director of national intelligence. There was little or no reaction to the appointment of one of the leading terrorist commanders to the position of counter-terrorism czar. That might make sense, given the similarity between the official definitions of "terrorism" and "counter-terrorism."

Democracy Building Must Begin at Home

AUGUST 30, 2004

The U.S. presidential campaign only points up the severe democratic deficit in the world's most powerful state.

Americans can choose between major-party candidates who were born to wealth and political power, attended the same elite university, joined the same secret society that instructs members in the style and manners of the rulers, and are able to run because they are funded by much the same corporate powers—one of a great many illustrations of the fact that the United States, long involved in alleged "democracy-building" adventures around the world, desperately needs to revitalize the democratic process at home.

Consider health care, a leading domestic issue. Costs are exploding in the mostly privatized U.S. system, already far higher than in comparable societies and with relatively poor outcomes. Polls regularly show that the majority of Americans favor some form of national health insurance. But the prospect is regularly described as "politically impossible" or "lacking political support." The financial institutions and pharmaceutical industry oppose it. With the effective erosion of a democratic culture, it doesn't matter what the population wants.

Iraq is the main international issue for the United States. In Spain, when voters demanded that their troops be removed unless placed under UN authority, they were denounced for "appeasing terrorism." In essence that's been the position of the majority of Americans since shortly after the invasion. The difference is that in Spain people know what popular opinion is and are able to vote on the issue.

The U.S. electorate feels disenchanted, according to the Vanishing Voter Project at the John F. Kennedy School of Government. During the 2000 campaign, project director Thomas Patterson reported, "Americans' feeling of powerlessness has reached an alarming high," with 53 percent responding "only a little" or "none" to the question: "How much influence do you think that people like you have on what the government does?" The previous peak, thirty years ago, was 41 percent.

Disaffection is understandable, the research shows, given most voters' view that politicians will say anything to get elected and that rich contributors exert too much influence.

In 2004, more seems to be at stake and interest is greater, according to the project, but there is a continuation of the disengagement mainly on the part of the poor and working-class Americans, who simply do not feel they are represented. "The turnout gap between the top and bottom fourth by income is by far the largest among western democracies and has been widening," Patterson writes.

The genius of the current political system is to render policy irrelevant, with advertising and the media concentrating not on "issues" but on "qualities" like the candidates' style, personality, and other irrelevancies. The political parties devolve into marketing systems for candidates.

In dramatic contrast, Brazil, the second-largest country in the hemisphere, held an authentic democratic election in 2002. The organized voters elected Luiz Inácio Lula da Silva, a person from the ranks of the working class and the poor, the overwhelming majority of the population. The campaign overcame barriers far higher than in the United States: a repressive state, tremendous inequality and concentration of wealth and media power, and extreme hostility of international capital and its institutions.

The election was won by mass popular organizations, which don't show up once every four years to push a lever, but are working every day, at grassroots levels, on local issues, regional government, and major policy issues.

In the United States, the Greens are concerned with long-term development of an electoral alternative of a kind that has succeeded in countries with a more functional democracy than here. But the Greens lack the support in the corporate sector that is necessary to compete in U.S. elections, just as someone who manufactures cars at home lacks the resources to compete with General Motors.

Ralph Nader has used the (rather artificial) glare of electoral politics to raise important issues not on the corporate agenda of either major party. But he's seen as a spoiler, fronting for Bush (hardly Nader's intention), which discredits him and the excellent organizations that he has founded.

Beyond the alternative candidates is the immediate real-world issue of Bush versus Kerry. At present, Bush has a substantial funding advantage over Kerry, thanks to the extraordinary gifts he lavishes on the superrich and the corporate sector, and his stellar record in demolishing the progressive legislation that has resulted from intense popular struggle over many years. And Bush will probably win unless a very powerful popular mobilization overcomes these enormous and usually decisive advantages.

The people around Bush are likely to cause very serious, perhaps irreparable, harm if given another term in office.

The prospect of a government that serves popular interests is being dismantled here.

Those who act to renew the Bush agenda are, in effect, telling people, "We don't care whether you have a better chance to receive health care or to support your elderly mother; or whether there will be a physical environment in which your children might have a decent life; or a world in which we may escape destruction as a result of the violence that is inspired by the Bush-Cheney-Rumsfeld-Wolfowitz-etc. crowd; and on, and on."

Revitalization of a functioning democratic culture in the United States matters a great deal to sensible people, and surely to the potential victims at home and abroad. And the same is true of the much narrower question that arises in the voting booths in November (2004).

The Disconnect in American Democracy

OCTOBER 27, 2004

The U.S. presidential race, impassioned almost to the point of hysteria, hardly represents healthy democratic impulses.

Americans are encouraged to vote, but not to participate more meaningfully in the political arena. Essentially the election is yet another method of marginalizing the population. A huge propaganda campaign is mounted to get people to focus on these personalized quadrennial extravaganzas and to think, "That's politics." But it isn't. It's only a small part of politics.

The population has been carefully excluded from political activity, and not by accident. An enormous amount of work has gone into that disenfranchisement. During the 1960s the outburst of popular participation in democracy terrified sectors of privilege and power, which mounted a fierce countercampaign, taking many forms, until today.

Bush and Kerry can run because they're funded by similar concentrations of private power. Both candidates understand that the election is supposed to stay away from issues. They are creatures of the public relations industry, which keeps the public out of the election process. Their task is to focus attention on the candidate's "qualities," not policies. Is he a leader? A nice guy? Voters end up endorsing an image, not a platform.

The regular vocation of the industries that sell candidates every few years is to sell commodities. Everyone who has turned on a TV set is aware that business devotes enormous efforts to undermine the markets of abstract theory, in which informed consumers make rational choices. An ad does not convey information, as it would in a market system; rather, it relies on deceit and illusions to create uninformed consumers who will make irrational choices. Much the same methods are used to undermine democracy by keeping the electorate uninformed and mired in delusion.

Last month (September 2004) a Gallup Poll asked Americans why they're voting for either Bush or Kerry. From a multiple-choice list, a mere 6 percent of Bush voters and 13 percent of Kerry voters picked the candidates' "agendas/ideas/platforms/goals." That's how the political system prefers it. Often the issues that are most on people's minds don't enter at all clearly into the debate.

A new report by the Chicago Council on Foreign Relations, which regularly monitors American attitudes on international issues, illustrates the disconnect.

A considerable majority of Americans favor "working within the United Nations, even when it adopts policies that the United States does not like." Most Americans also believe that "countries should have the right to go to war on their own only if they (have) strong evidence that they are in imminent danger of being attacked," thus rejecting the bipartisan consensus on "pre-emptive war."

On Iraq, polls by the Program on International Policy Attitudes show that a majority of Americans favor letting the United Nations take the lead in issues of reconstruction and political transition in that country. Last March (2004) Spanish voters actually could vote on these matters.

It is notable that Americans hold these and similar views (say, on the International Criminal Court or the Kyoto Protocol) in virtual isolation: They rarely hear them in campaign speeches and probably regard them as idiosyncratic. At the same time, the level of activism for social change may be higher than ever in the United States. But it's disorganized. Nobody knows what's happening on the other side of town.

By contrast, consider the fundamentalist Christians. Earlier this month (October 2004) in Jerusalem, Pat Robertson said that he would start a third party if Bush and the Republicans waver in support for Israel. That's a serious threat because he might be able to mobilize tens of millions of evangelical Christians who already form a significant political force, thanks to extensive work over decades on numerous issues, and with candidates at levels from school board to president.

The presidential race isn't devoid of issue-oriented activism. During the primaries, before the main event fully gears up, candidates can raise issues and help organize popular support for them, thereby influencing campaigns to some extent. After the primaries, mere statements make a minimal impact without a significant organization behind them.

The urgent task for those who want to shift policy in a progressive direction—often in close conformity to majority opinion—is to grow and become strong enough so that they can't be ignored by centers of power. Forces for change that have come up from the grass roots and shaken the society to its core include the labor movement, the civil rights movement, the peace movement, the women's movement and others, cultivated by steady, dedicated work at all levels, every day, not just once every four years.

But we can't ignore the elections. We should recognize that one of the two groups now contending for power happens to be extremist and dangerous, and has already caused plenty of trouble and could cause plenty more.

Since I am often asked, I've taken the same position as in 2000. If you are in a swing state, you should vote to keep the worst guys out. If it's another state, do what you feel is best. There are many considerations.

Bush and his administration are publicly committed to dismantling and destroying whatever progressive legislation and social welfare has been won by popular struggles over the past century. Internationally, they are calling for dominating the world by military force, including even the "ownership of space" to expand monitoring and first-strike capabilities.

So in the election, sensible choices have to be made. But they are secondary to serious political action. The main task is to create a genuinely responsive democratic culture, and that effort goes on before and after electoral extravaganzas, whatever their outcome.

"We" Are Good

NOVEMBER 24, 2004

In discussion of international relations, the fundamental principle is that "we are good"—"we" being the government, on the totalitarian principle that state and people are one. "We" are benevolent, seeking peace and justice, though there may be errors in practice. "We" are foiled by villains who can't rise to our exalted level.

The events of recent weeks—including the U.S. elections, the attack on Fallujah, and the shifts in President Bush's cabinet—dramatize the operative principle and, on an immediate practical level, ratchet up the peril of war and terror.

Washington's military policies "carry an appreciable risk of ultimate doom," write strategic analysts John D. Steinbruner and Nancy Gallagher in the summer (2004) issue of *Daedalus*, the journal of the American Academy of Arts and Sciences, not given to hyperbole. The authors go on to express the hope that the threat will be countered by a coalition of peace-loving nations led by China. Matters have reached a pretty pass when informed commentators are compelled to conclude that peace must rely on China. The implicit critique of the state of American democracy is harsh and bitter.

Even apart from literal threats to survival of the species, the urgency is apparent. In Iraq, 100,000 civilians may have died as a direct or indirect consequence of the U.S.-led invasion in March (2003), according to a study in the *Lancet* led by a research team at Johns Hopkins University.[1]

Washington and London discounted the study. Accordingly, when it is referred to in the small print, its name becomes "the controversial study."

That's not counting the recent deaths in Fallujah. The assault began as U.S. forces and Iraqi troops seized Fallujah General Hospital, described by officers as a "propaganda weapon for the militants . . . with its stream of reports of civilian casualties," according to the *New York Times*. Another *Times* story reported, "Patients and hospital employees were rushed out of rooms and ordered to sit or lie on the floor while troops tied their hands behind their backs."

The attack on the hospital is in gross violation of the Geneva Conventions, part of the "supreme Law of the Land" and the foundation of modern humanitarian law. The War Crimes Act of 1996 (passed by a Republican Congress) carries the death penalty for commanders responsible for "grave breaches" of the Geneva Conventions.

The War Crimes Act also surfaced with the appointment of White House counsel Alberto Gonzales as attorney general. In January 2002, in a memo to the president about new measures in the "war on terrorism," Gonzales advised Bush to circumvent the Geneva Conventions—which thereby "substantially reduces the threat of domestic criminal prosecution under the War Crimes Act."[2]

Disregard for international law is a point of pride for Bush's people. Condoleezza Rice, Bush's appointee as secretary of state, outlined her views in the January 2000 issue of *Foreign Affairs*, where she condemned the "reflexive appeal . . . to notions of international law and norms, and the belief that the support of many states—or even better, of institutions like the United Nations—is essential to the legitimate exercise of power."

We have a fairly clear idea of what Bush's planners want, but what we can expect depends on circumstances, including those we bring into existence. That should include creating—and in part re-creating—a functioning democratic culture where the public enters into planning in a meaningful way, and where we accept the fundamental moral principle that we apply the same standards to ourselves that we apply to others.

NOTES

1. For more recent estimates, see note 2, page 17.
2. The Military Commissions Act of 2006 effectively immunizes Bush administration officials from the War Crimes Act, among other features of what may be the most shameful piece of legislation in American history.

Imperial Presidency and Its Consequences

DECEMBER 22, 2004

What happens in the United States has an enormous impact on the rest of the world—and conversely. International events constrain what even the most powerful state can do. They also influence the domestic U.S. component of the "second superpower," as the *New York Times* described world public opinion after the huge protests before the Iraq invasion.

By contrast, serious U.S. protest took years to develop against the Vietnam War, launched in 1962 and brutal and barbaric from the start. The world has changed since then—as almost always, not because of gifts from benevolent leaders, but through deeply committed popular struggle, far too late in developing, but ultimately effective.

The world is in awful shape today, but far better than yesterday, with regard to unwillingness to tolerate aggression, and in many other ways that we tend to take for granted. The lessons from that transformation should be uppermost in our minds.

It's not surprising that as the population becomes more civilized, power systems become more extreme in their efforts to control the "great beast" (as Alexander Hamilton called the people). The great beast is indeed frightening.

The Bush administration's conception of presidential sovereignty is so extreme that it has even drawn unprecedented criticism from the most sober and respected journals. In the post-9/11 world, the administration behaves as if constitutional and other norms are suspended, writes Sanford Levinson, a law professor at the University of Texas, in the summer (2004) issue of *Daedalus*, the journal of the American Academy of Arts and Sciences.

The anything-goes-during-wartime rationale might be characterized as "There exists no norm that is applicable to chaos."

The quote, Levinson points out, is from Carl Schmitt, the leading German philosopher of law during the Nazi period, whom Levinson describes as "the true éminence grise of the (Bush) administration." As advised by White House counsel (now attorney general designate) Alberto Gonzales, the administration has articulated "a view of presidential authority that is all too close to the power that Schmitt was willing to accord his own Führer," Levinson writes.

One rarely hears such words from the heart of the Establishment.

These conceptions of imperial presidential authority underlie administration policies. The invasion of Iraq was initially justified as an act of so-called anticipatory self-defense. The attack violated the principles of the Nuremberg Tribunal, a basis for the UN Charter, which declared that initiation of a war of aggression is "the supreme international crime differing only from other war crimes in that it contains within itself the accumulated evil of the whole"—hence the war crimes in Fallujah and Abu Ghraib, the crimes of the insurgency, the doubling of acute malnutrition among children since the invasion (now at the level of Burundi, far higher than Haiti or Uganda), and all the rest of the atrocities.

Last spring (2004), after it was reported that U.S. Department of Justice lawyers had tried to demonstrate that the president could authorize torture, Yale Law School Dean Harold Koh told the *Financial Times*, "The notion that the president has the constitutional power to permit torture is like saying he has the constitutional power to commit genocide."

The president's legal advisers, and the new attorney general, should have little difficulty arguing that the president does indeed have that right—if the second superpower permits him to exercise it.[1]

The administration labors to find a way to free high officials from accountability. The sacred doctrine of self-immunization is sure to apply to the trial of Saddam Hussein (at this writing, charges may even be filed in Iraq next week against former members of his government and perhaps against Saddam himself). When Bush, Prime Minister Tony Blair, and other worthies in government and commentary lament over Saddam's terrible crimes, they always bravely omit the words: "with our help, because we did not care."

"All efforts are being made to have a tribunal that appears independent but whose U.S. handlers can ensure is controlled, to avoid calling into question the role of the United States and other western powers who previously supported the regime," Cherif Bassiouni, a DePaul University law professor and expert on the Iraqi legal system, told *Le Monde diplomatique* (January 2004). "This makes it look like victor's vengeance." We hardly need to be told.

What is the best response to the situation? In the United States we enjoy a legacy of great privilege and freedom, remarkable by comparative and historical standards. We can abandon that legacy and take the easy way of pessimism: Everything is hopeless, so I'll quit.

Or we can make use of that legacy to further a democratic

culture in which the public plays some role in determining policies, not only in politics but also in the crucial economic arena.

These are hardly radical ideas. They were articulated clearly, for example, by John Dewey, the leading twentieth-century U.S. social philosopher, who pointed out that until "industrial feudalism" is replaced by "industrial democracy," politics will remain "the shadow cast by big business over society."

Dewey was drawing from a long tradition of thought and action that had developed independently in working-class culture from the origins of the U.S. industrial revolution, near Boston. Such ideas remain just below the surface, and they can become a living part of our societies, cultures and institutions. But like other victories for justice and freedom over the centuries, nothing will happen by itself. One of the clearest lessons of history, including recent history, is that rights are not granted; they are won.

NOTES

1. The Clinton administration effectively claimed that right, when it excluded itself from the World Court proceedings brought by Yugoslavia against NATO. Yugoslavia had invoked the Genocide Convention, but the Clinton administration argued before the Court that when the U.S. ratified the Convention (after forty years), it added a reservation stating that it was not applicable to the U.S. unless Congress so determined. The ICJ accepted that argument, correctly, permitting the U.S. to withdraw from the proceedings. U.S. self-immunization is routine. The U.S. rarely ratifies human rights and other conventions, but when it does there is usually—maybe always—a reservation excluding itself. In the

case of the Torture convention, Levinson notes, the U.S. accepted it only after the Senate had rewritten it to make it more "interrogation friendly," in his words. There are many other illustrations of explicit self-exclusion from international law.

The Iraq Debacle and International Order

FEBRUARY 1, 2005

Few questions are more important today than the propriety of the use of force, underscored all too bloodily by the scenes of suffering from Iraq. Beyond the human toll, the U.S.-led invasion and occupation of Iraq violated a fragile international compact, enacted in the aftermath of the horrors of the World War II years, to outlaw the resort to force in international affairs. That violation, along with the ascendancy of terrorism, has compelled the United Nations to address again just when force is justified. The backdrop for the debate is the deteriorating situation in Iraq.

A government's use of force is almost always accompanied by professions of benign intent. So it is in Iraq. As all other official pretexts have collapsed, the Washington PR system shifted to the claim that the mission there is to install a democracy that will reform the country and then perhaps the region. It takes impressive faith in power to assume that because our leaders have announced their vision of democracy for Iraq after the collapse of official pretexts, they really mean it.

As the Iraqi elections demonstrate, the United States has already been forced to concede some of the formal mechanisms of democracy, which is a good thing, but to concede true democracy and sovereign rights in Iraq is virtually inconceivable—without broad-based pressure from American and Iraqi citizens.

Consider what a sovereign, independent Iraq's policies might be. With a Shiite majority, Iraq may carry forward earlier efforts to restore relatively friendly relations with Iran. That might well stir up initiatives within the largely Shiite areas nearby in Saudi Arabia to join an informal Shiite-dominated region—which happens to include two-thirds of the world's estimated hydrocarbon reserves.

Control of those reserves has been a crucial policy concern throughout the post–World War II period, even more so in today's evolving tripolar world, with its threat that Europe and Asia might move toward greater independence. A firm hand on the spigot provides "critical leverage" over Asian and European economies, as Zbigniew Brzezinski observed in the *National Interest*, Winter 2003/2004, echoing well-established principles. Furthermore, an independent Iraq would eventually rearm and possibly even develop weapons of mass destruction to confront those of the regional enemy, U.S.-backed Israel.

The United States is hardly likely to sit by and watch these developments. Its likely reaction follows from the policies that have dealt yet another serious blow to the post–World War II consensus on the use of force.

The UN Charter opens by expressing the determination of the signatories "to save succeeding generations from the scourge of war, which twice in our lifetime has brought untold sorrow to mankind" and which by then also threatened total destruction, as all participants knew—but also knew they could not mention. The words "atomic" or "nuclear" do not appear in the UN Charter.

A war of aggression was seen as the supreme international crime. Formally, the consensus remains. It is usually not rejected explicitly. Rather, it is ignored.

The official retraction of the consensus took place quite

recently, during the 1990s, when the United States formally arrogated to itself the freedom to resort to force, irrespective of attack. The Clinton doctrine was that the United States reserves the right to use military force "unilaterally when necessary," to defend vital interests such as "ensuring uninhibited access to key markets, energy supplies and strategic resources," according to a 1997 Pentagon report to Congress. The Bush administration consolidates and extends the position that the United States has the unilateral right to resort to force when it chooses to do so.

The rationale for this imperial stance runs as deep as American history. The worldview, as historian William Earl Weeks writes in *John Quincy Adams and American Global Empire*, is based on "the assumption of the unique moral virtue of the United States, the assertion of its mission to redeem the world" by spreading its professed ideals and the " 'American way of life,' and the faith in the nation's divinely ordained destiny." This theological framework reduces policy issues to a choice between Good and Evil, thus undercutting reasoned debate and fending off the threat of democracy.

The issue of the legitimacy of the use of force was addressed last November (2004) by a high-level UN panel convened by Secretary-General Kofi Annan. The panel reiterated the UN Charter: Without Security Council authorization to the contrary, force is restricted only to self-defense against armed attack.

Washington does not accept the idea that the United States should adhere to such a standard—a fact that should concern all of us who enjoy privilege and freedom, with their attendant responsibility.

In his new book *War Law: Understanding International Law and Armed Conflict* (2005), international legal scholar Michael

Byers raises the question of how we might survive "the tension between a world that still wants a sustainable legal system and a superpower that hardly seems to care." It is a question that cannot be lightly disregarded.

"Democracy Promotion" in the Middle East

MARCH 2, 2005

So-called democracy promotion has become the leading theme of declared U.S. policy in the Middle East.

The project has a background. There is a "strong line of continuity" in the post–Cold War period, writes Thomas Carothers, director of the Democracy and Rule of Law Program of the Carnegie Endowment for International Peace, in his new book *Critical Mission: Essays on Democracy Promotion* (2004).

"Where democracy appears to fit in well with U.S. security and economic interests, the United States promotes democracy," Carothers concludes. "Where democracy clashes with other significant interests, it is downplayed or even ignored."

Carothers served in the Reagan State Department on "democracy enhancement" projects in Latin America during the 1980s and wrote a history of them, drawing essentially the same conclusions. Similar actions and pretensions hold for earlier periods as well and are characteristic of other dominant powers.

The strong line of continuity, and the power interests that sustain it, affect recent events in the Middle East, pointing up the real substance of the posture of "promoting democracy."

The continuity is illustrated by the nomination of John Negroponte as the first director of national intelligence. The arc of Negroponte's career ranges from Honduras, where as Reagan's ambassador he oversaw the Contra terrorist forces' war against Nicaragua, to Iraq, where as Bush's ambassador he briefly presided over another exercise in alleged democracy development—experience that can inform his new duties to help combat terror and promote liberty. Orwell would not have known whether to laugh or to weep.

In Iraq, the January (2005) elections were successful and praiseworthy. However, the main success is being reported only marginally: The United States was compelled to allow them to take place. That is a real triumph, not of the bombthrowers, but of nonviolent resistance by the people, secular as well as Islamist, for whom Grand Ayatollah Ali al-Sistani is a symbol.

Despite U.S.-U.K. foot-dragging, Sistani demanded speedy elections, reflecting popular determination to achieve freedom and independence, and some form of democratic rights. The nonviolent resistance continued until the United States (and the United Kingdom, trailing obediently behind) had no recourse but to allow the elections. The doctrinal machinery then went into high gear to present the elections as a U.S. initiative.

In line with the "strong line of continuity" and its institutional roots, we can anticipate that Washington will not readily tolerate political outcomes that it opposes, particularly in such a crucial region of the world.

Iraqis voted with the hope of ending the occupation. In January (2005), a preelection poll in Iraq, reported by Brookings Institution analysts in the *New York Times*, found that 69 percent of Shiites, and 82 percent of Sunnis, favored "near-term U.S. withdrawal." But Blair, Rice, and others have been explicit in rejecting any timetable for withdrawal—that is, putting it off into the indefinite future—until the occupying armies complete their "mission," namely, to bring democracy by forcing the elected government to conform to U.S. demands, in accord with the "strong line of continuity."

Hastening a U.S.-U.K. withdrawal depends not only on Iraqis but also on the willingness of the American and British electorates to compel their governments to accept Iraqi sovereignty.

As events unfold in Iraq, the United States continues to maintain a militant posture toward Iran. The recent leaks about U.S. Special Forces on the ground in Iran, whether true or false, inflame the situation.

A genuine threat is that in recent years the United States has dispatched more than one-hundred advanced jet bombers to Israel, with clear announcements that they are capable of bombing Iran, updated versions of the planes that Israel used to bomb the Iraqi nuclear reactor in 1981—incidentally, initiating Saddam Hussein's nuclear weapons program, so the evidence indicates.

It's a matter of conjecture, but the saber rattling may serve two purposes: to provoke the Iranian leadership to become more repressive, thus encouraging popular resistance; and to intimidate U.S. rivals in Europe and Asia from pursuing diplomatic and economic initiatives toward Iran. The hard line has already scared off some European investments in Iran, for fear of U.S. retaliation, reports Matthew Karnitschnig in the *Wall Street Journal*.

Another development being hailed as a triumph of democracy promotion is the Sharon-Abbas cease-fire. The news of the agreement is welcome: better no killing than killing, temporarily. Take a close look at the cease-fire terms, however. The only substantive element is that Palestinian resistance, even against the occupying army, must cease.

Nothing could delight U.S.-Israeli hawks more than complete peace, which would enable them to pursue, unhindered, the policies of takeover of the valuable land and resources of the West Bank, and huge infrastructure projects to break up the remaining Palestinian territories into unviable cantons.

U.S.-backed Israeli depredations in the occupied territories have been the core issue of the conflict for years, but the cease-fire agreement contains not a word about them. The Abbas government accepted the agreement—perhaps, one might argue, because it's the best they can do as long as Israel and the United States reject a political settlement. It might be added that the U.S. intransigence can continue only as long as the American population allows.

I'd like to be optimistic about the agreement and leap at any straw in the wind, but so far I see nothing real.

For Washington there is indeed "a strong line of continuity," much as Carothers ruefully concludes: democracy and the rule of law are acceptable if and only if they serve official strategic and economic objectives. But American public attitudes on Iraq and Israel-Palestine run counter to government policy, according to polls. Therefore the question presents itself whether a genuine democracy promotion might best begin within the United States.

The Universality of Human Rights

APRIL 7, 2005

In recent years, moral philosophy and cognitive science have explored what seem to be deep-seated moral intuitions—perhaps the very foundations of moral judgment.

These inquiries focus on invented examples that often reveal surprising cross-cultural uniformities of judgment, in children as well as adults. To illustrate, I will instead take a real example that carries us to the issue of universality of human rights.

In 1991, Lawrence Summers, later President Clinton's treasury secretary and now president of Harvard University, was chief economist of the World Bank. In an internal memo, Summers demonstrated that the Bank should encourage polluting industries to move to the poorest countries.

The reason is that "the measurement of the costs of health impairing pollution depends on the foregone earnings from increased morbidity and mortality," Summers wrote: "From this point of view, a given amount of health impairing pollution should be done in the country with the lowest cost, which will be the country with the lowest wages. I think the economic logic behind dumping a load of toxic waste in the lowest wage country is impeccable and we should face up to that."

Summers pointed out that any "moral reasons" or "social concerns" about such a move "could be turned around and used more or less effectively against every Bank proposal for liberalization."

The memo was leaked, and led to a furious reaction, typified by José Lutzenberger, Brazil's secretary of the environment, who wrote to Summers, "Your reasoning is perfectly logical but totally insane." Those who agree with Lutzenberger's conclusion face a clear and important task. If a perfectly logical argument leads to a totally insane conclusion, then the problem must lie with the premises, in particular, the rejection of "moral reasons" or "social concerns." Then follows another task, if Summers is right that such a move can be used against all World Bank proposals for "liberalization"—that is, implementation of the "Washington consensus." The conclusion seems obvious without spelling it out. It is perhaps of some interest that this reasoning, hardly more than elementary logic, appears to have been ignored within mainstream opinion, neither refuted nor pursued.

The modern standard for such questions is the Universal Declaration of Human Rights, adopted by the UN General Assembly in 1948.

Article 25 declares, "Everyone has the right to a standard of living adequate for the health and well-being of himself and of his family, including food, clothing, housing and medical care and necessary social services, and the right to security in the event of unemployment, sickness, disability, widowhood, old age or other lack of livelihood in circumstances beyond his control."

In almost the same words, these provisions have been reaffirmed in enabling conventions of the General Assembly and in international agreements on the "right to development."

It seems reasonably clear that this formulation of universal human rights rejects the impeccable logic of the World Bank's chief economist as profoundly immoral if not insane—which was, in fact, the virtually universal judgment.

I stress the word "virtually." Western culture condemns some nations as "relativists," who interpret the Universal Declaration selectively. Systematically ignored, however, is that one of the principal relativists happens to be the world's most powerful state, the leader of the self-designated "enlightened states."

A month ago (March 2005), the U.S. State Department issued its annual report on human rights. "Promoting human rights is not just an element of our foreign policy, it is the bedrock of our policy and our foremost concern," said Paula Dobriansky, undersecretary of state for democracy and global affairs.

Dobriansky was deputy assistant secretary of state for human rights and humanitarian affairs in the Reagan and Bush I administrations, and in that capacity she sought to dispel what she called the "myth" that " 'economic and social rights' constitute human rights." This position has been frequently reiterated and underlies Washington's veto of the "right to development" and its consistent refusal to accept human rights conventions.

The government may reject the Universal Declaration's provisions. But the U.S. population disagrees. One example is public reaction to the recently proposed federal budget, as surveyed by the Program on International Policy Attitudes at the University of Maryland.

The public calls for sharp cuts in military spending along with sharply increased spending for education, medical research, job training, conservation, renewable energy, and other social programs, as well as for the United Nations and economic and humanitarian aid, along with the reversal of Bush's tax cuts for the wealthy. Overall, popular preferences are virtually the opposite of the government's budget decisions.

There is, rightly, much international concern about the rapidly expanding U.S. trade and budget deficits. Closely related is the growing democratic deficit, not just in the United States but in the West generally.

Wealth and power have every reason to want the public largely removed from policy choices and implementation— also a matter of concern, quite apart from its relation to the universality of human rights.

We have just passed the twenty-fifth anniversary of the assassination of Archbishop Oscar Romero of El Salvador, known as a "voice for the voiceless," and the fifteenth anniversary of the murder of six leading Latin American intellectuals, who were Jesuit priests, also in El Salvador.

The events framed the hideous decade of the 1980s in Central America. Romero and the Jesuit intellectuals were murdered by security forces armed and trained by Washington. Among those responsible are leading figures of the present administration or their immediate mentors.

The archbishop was assassinated shortly after he wrote to President Carter, pleading with him not to send aid to the military junta in El Salvador, which will "sharpen the repression that has been unleashed against the people's organizations fighting to defend their most fundamental human rights." State terror escalated, always with U.S. support and with Western silence and complicity.

Similar atrocities are taking place right now, at the hands of military forces armed and trained by Washington, with the support of its Western allies: for example, in Colombia, the hemisphere's leading human-rights violator for many years, and leading recipient of U.S. military aid through the same period, illustrating another "strong line of continuity," well documented.

It appears that last year (2004) Colombia retained its record of killing more labor activists than the rest of world combined. In February (2005), in a town that had declared itself a "peace community" in Colombia's civil war, the military reportedly massacred eight people, including a town leader and three children.

I mention these scattered examples to remind ourselves that we are not merely engaged in seminars on abstract principles, or discussing remote cultures that we do not comprehend. We are speaking of ourselves, and the moral and intellectual values of the privileged communities in which we live. If we do not like what we see if we look into the mirror honestly, we have every opportunity to do something about it.

Dr. Strangelove Meets the Age of Terror

APRIL 28, 2005

Next week a United Nations conference of 180 signatory nations will review the Nuclear Non-Proliferation Treaty (NPT), commonly regarded as the foundation of any serious hope to avoid the catastrophe that is virtually guaranteed by the logic of nuclear weapons.

"The NPT has never seemed weaker or its future less certain," Thomas Graham, former U.S. special representative for arms control, nonproliferation, and disarmament and author of *Common Sense on Weapons of Mass Destruction* (2004), writes in this month's (April 2005) issue of *Current History*.

If the treaty should fail in the coming weeks, Graham warns, a "nuclear nightmare world" may become reality.

Like other analysts, Graham recognizes that the primary threat to the NPT is U.S. government policy, though the other nuclear states share responsibility.

The treaty was a compact in which the nuclear powers pledged to take "good faith" efforts to eliminate nuclear weapons, the crucial Article VI. None have, and the Bush administration has gone beyond, declaring that it no longer accepts that core provision of the NPT, and is now even seeking to develop new nuclear weapons.

The NPT was also based on commitment to several additional treaties: the Comprehensive Test Ban Treaty, rejected by the Republican Senate in 1999, and declared off the agenda by President George W. Bush; the Anti-Ballistic Missile Treaty, which Bush rescinded; and, probably most important, a verifiable Fissile Material Cutoff Treaty, which, Graham writes, would block the dread threat of adding "more nuclear bomb material to the vast amount already existing."

Last November (2004) the UN Committee on Disarmament voted in favor of the treaty by 147 to 1. The unilateral U.S. vote is, in effect, a veto. It provides some further insight into the ranking of survival of the species on the list of priorities of government planners.

Earlier the Bush administration sent point man John Bolton to inform Europe that lengthy negotiations on enforcing a bioweapons ban were over, because they were not "in the best interests of the United States," thereby increasing the threat of bioterror.

That is consistent with Bolton's forthright stand: "When the United States leads, the United Nations will follow. When it suits our interests to do so, we will do so. When it does not suit our interests, we will not."

It is only natural that he should be nominated to be America's ambassador to the United Nations, in a calculated insult to Europe and to the world.

Under current policies "a nuclear exchange is ultimately inevitable," Michael MccGwire, former NATO planner, warns in the January (2005) issue of *International Affairs*, the journal of Britain's Royal Institute of International Affairs. "By comparison with global warming, the cost of eliminating nuclear weapons would be small," MccGwire writes. "But the catastrophic results of global nuclear war would greatly exceed those of progressive climate change, because the effects would be instantaneous and could not be mitigated. The irony of the situation is that it is in our power to eliminate the threat of global nuclear war, but climate change cannot be evaded."

MccGwire's warnings are echoed on this side of the Atlantic by Sam Nunn, formerly a Democratic senator and chairman of the Senate Armed Services Committee, who has been a leading figure in arms control and efforts to reduce the threat of nuclear war. "The chances of an accidental, mistaken or unauthorized nuclear attack might be increasing," Nunn wrote in the *Financial Times* in December (2004). As a result of policy choices that leave "America's survival [dependent on] the accuracy of Russia's warning systems and its command and control . . . we are running an unnecessary risk of an Armageddon of our own making."

In the background of Nunn's remarks is the sharp expansion of U.S. military programs, which tilt the strategic balance in ways that make Russia "more likely to launch upon warning of an attack, without waiting to see if the warning is accurate." The threat is enhanced, he adds, by the fact that "the Russian early-warning system is in serious disrepair and more likely to give a false warning of incoming missiles."

A related concern is that nuclear weapons may sooner or later fall into the hands of terrorist groups, made more likely by the fact that, as a deterrent against U.S. threats, Russia must maintain its own nuclear arsenal, scattered across its vast territory, with materials often in transit. "This perpetual motion creates a serious vulnerability, because transportation is the Achilles' heel of nuclear-weapons security," notes Bruce Blair, president of the Washington-based Center for Defense Information and a former Minuteman launch officer. Blair invokes the altogether plausible possibility of "terrorists grabbing such a weapon as it shuttles between deployment fields and factories."

The risk extends beyond Russia, he adds. "The early-warning and control problems plaguing Pakistan, India and other nuclear proliferators are even more acute [and], as these nations move toward hair-trigger stances for their nuclear missiles, the terrorist threat to them will grow in parallel," Blair writes. All of this, he concludes, constitutes "an accident waiting to happen."

State terror and other forms of threat and use of force have brought the world very close to the edge of nuclear annihilation. The UN would be wise to heed the call issued by Bertrand Russell and Albert Einstein fifty years ago: "Here, then, is the problem which we present to you, stark and dreadful and inescapable: Shall we put an end to the human race, or shall mankind renounce war?"

The Social Security Non-Crisis

MAY 29, 2005

In the debate over Social Security, President Bush's handlers have already won some victories, at least in the short term.

Bush and Karl Rove, his deputy chief of staff, have succeeded in convincing most of the U.S. population, including more than two-thirds of college students, that there is a serious problem with Social Security, which opens the way for considering the administration's program of private accounts instead of relying on the public pension system. The public has been frightened, much as it was by the imminent threat of Saddam Hussein and his weapons of mass destruction. The pressure on politicians is rising as leaders in the U.S. House of Representatives hope to draft Social Security legislation by next month (June 2005).

For perspective, perhaps it should be noted that Social Security is one of the least generous public pension systems among advanced countries, according to a new report by the Organisation for Economic Co-operation and Development.

The Bush administration wants to "reform" Social Security—meaning dismantle it. A huge government-media propaganda campaign has concocted a "fiscal crisis" that is mostly imaginary. If some problem does arise in the distant future, it could be overcome by trivial measures, such as raising the cap on the regressive payroll tax.

The official story is that the baby boomers are going to

impose a greater burden on the system because the number of working people relative to the elderly will decline, which is true. But what happened to the baby boomers when they were zero to twenty? Weren't working people taking care of them? And it was a much poorer society then.

In the 1960s the demographics caused a problem but hardly a crisis. The bulge was met by a big increase in expenditures in schools and other facilities for children. The problem wasn't huge when the baby boomers were zero to twenty, so why when they're seventy to ninety?

The relevant number is what's called the dependency ratio of working people to population. That ratio reached its lowest point in 1965. It won't reach that point again until 2080, according to Social Security Administration figures. Projections that far ahead are meaningless.

Furthermore, any fiscal problem that might arise in caring for the elderly boomers has already been paid for, by the payroll tax rise of 1983, designed for this purpose. And by the time the last boomer has died, the society will be far richer, with each worker producing far greater wealth.

In other words, we're already past that crisis. Anything that comes is just a matter of one or another kind of adjustment.

Meanwhile a very real fiscal crisis is looming: namely, medical care. The United States has one of the most inefficient systems in the industrialized world, with per capita costs far higher than other nations and among the worst health outcomes. The system is privatized, one reason why it's so inefficient, with administrative costs far higher than Medicare or public programs in other countries, among many other severe flaws inherent in privatized health care.

But "reforming" the health-care system is not on the agenda. So we face an apparent paradox: The real and very serious fiscal crisis is no crisis, and the non-crisis requires drastic action to undermine an efficient system that is quite sound.

Rational observers will seek differences between the Social Security and health-care systems that might explain the paradox.

Some of the reasons seem clear. You can't go after a health system under the control of insurance companies and pharmaceutical corporations. That system is immune, and will remain so even if it is causing tremendous financial problems (quite apart from the human cost), until some other sector of concentrated power, probably manufacturing industry, throws its weight into the fray on this issue—or better, until formal democratic institutions function sufficiently well for public opinion to become a factor in policy formation.

A further reason is that Social Security is of little value for the rich though it is crucial for survival for working people, the poor, their dependents, and the disabled. And as a government program, it has such low administrative costs that it offers nothing to financial institutions. It benefits only the "underlying population," not the "substantial citizens," to borrow Thorstein Veblen's acid terminology.

The medical system, however, works very well for the people who matter. Health care is effectively rationed by wealth, and enormous profits flow to private power thanks to management practices geared to profit, not health care. The underlying population can be treated with lectures on responsibility.

The U.S. Congress has recently enacted bankruptcy reform that tightens the stranglehold on the underlying population. About half of U.S. bankruptcies result from medical bills.

Opinion and official policy are once again in conflict. As in the past, most Americans favor national health insurance. To cite just one of many illustrations, in a 2003 Washington Post–ABC News poll, 80 percent regarded universal health care as "more important than holding down taxes."

Quite apart from these considerations, Social Security is based on an extremely dangerous principle: that you should care whether the disabled widow across town has food to eat. The Social Security "reformers" would rather have you concentrate on maximizing your own consumption of goods and subordinating yourself to power. Caring for other people, and taking community responsibility for things like health and retirement—that's deeply subversive.

The Hidden Agenda in the Iraq War

JULY 1, 2005

In his June 28 (2005) speech, President Bush asserted that the invasion of Iraq was undertaken as part of "a global war against terror" that the United States is waging. In reality, as anticipated, the invasion increased the threat of terror, perhaps significantly.

Half-truths, misinformation, and hidden agendas have characterized official pronouncements about U.S. war motives in Iraq from the very beginning. The recent revelations about the rush to war in Iraq stand out all the more starkly amid the chaos that ravages the country and threatens the region and, indeed, the world.

In 2002 the United States and United Kingdom proclaimed the right to invade Iraq because it was developing weapons of mass destruction. That was the "single question," as stressed constantly by Bush, Prime Minister Blair, and associates. It was also the sole basis on which Bush received congressional authorization to resort to force.

The answer to the "single question" was given shortly after the invasion, and reluctantly conceded: The weapons of mass destruction didn't exist. Scarcely missing a beat, the government and media doctrinal system concocted new pretexts and justifications for going to war.

"Americans do not like to think of themselves as aggressors, but raw aggression is what took place in Iraq," national security and intelligence analyst John Prados concluded after his careful, extensive review of the documentary record in his 2004 book *Hoodwinked*. Prados describes the Bush "scheme to convince America and the world that war with Iraq was necessary and urgent" as "a case study in government dishonesty . . . that required patently untrue public statements and egregious manipulation of intelligence."

The Downing Street memo, published on May 1 (2005) in the *Sunday Times* of London, and other newly available confidential documents have deepened the record of deceit.

The memo came from a meeting of Blair's war cabinet on July 23, 2002, in which Sir Richard Dearlove, head of British foreign intelligence, made the now-notorious assertion that "the intelligence and facts were being fixed around the policy" of going to war in Iraq.

The memo also quotes British Defense Secretary Geoff Hoon as saying that "the U.S. had already begun 'spikes of activity' to put pressure on the regime."

British journalist Michael Smith, who broke the story of the memo, has elaborated on its context and contents in subsequent articles. The "spikes of activity" apparently included a coalition air campaign meant to provoke Iraq into some act that could be portrayed as what the memo calls a "casus belli." Warplanes began bombing in southern Iraq in May 2002—10 tons that month, according to British government figures. A special "spike" started in late August (for a September total of 54.6 tons).

"In other words, Bush and Blair began their war not in March 2003, as everyone believed, but at the end of August 2002, six weeks before Congress approved military action against Iraq," Smith wrote.

The bombing was presented as defensive action to protect

coalition planes in the no-fly zone. Iraq protested to the United Nations but didn't fall into the trap of retaliating.[1]

For U.S.-U.K. planners, invading Iraq was a far higher priority than the "war on terror." That much is revealed by the reports of their own intelligence agencies. On the eve of the allied invasion, a classified report by the National Intelligence Council (NIC), the intelligence community's center for strategic thinking, "predicted that an American-led invasion of Iraq would increase support for political Islam and would result in a deeply divided Iraqi society prone to violent internal conflict," Douglas Jehl and David E. Sanger reported in the *New York Times* last September (2004).

In December 2004, Jehl reported a few weeks later, the NIC warned that "Iraq and other possible conflicts in the future could provide recruitment, training grounds, technical skills and language proficiency for a new class of terrorists who are 'professionalized' and for whom political violence becomes an end in itself."

The willingness of top planners to risk increase of terrorism does not of course indicate that they welcome such outcomes. Rather, they are simply not a high priority in comparison with other objectives, such as controlling the world's major energy resources.

If the United States can maintain its control over Iraq, with the world's second-largest known oil reserves, and right at the heart of the world's major energy supplies, that will enhance significantly its strategic power and influence over its major rivals in the tripolar world that has been taking shape for the past thirty years: U.S.-dominated North America, Europe, and Northeast Asia, linked to South and Southeast Asia economies.

It is a rational calculation, on the assumption that human survival is not particularly significant in comparison with short-term power and wealth. And that is nothing new. These themes resonate through history. The difference today in this age of nuclear weapons is only that the stakes are enormously higher.

NOTES

1. On the illegality of the no-fly zones, and the grim effects on civilians in earlier years, see von Sponeck, *A Different Kind of War* (2006).

The Legacy of Hiroshima and the Present Terror

AUGUST 2, 2005

This month's anniversary of the bombings of Hiroshima and Nagasaki prompts somber reflection and fervent hope that the horror may never be repeated. In the subsequent sixty years, those bombings have haunted the world's imagination but not so much as to curb the development and spread of vastly more lethal weapons of mass destruction.

A related concern, discussed in technical literature well before 9/11, is that nuclear weapons may sooner or later fall into the hands of terrorist groups.

The recent bombings in London (July 2005) are yet another reminder of how the cycle of attack and response could escalate, unpredictably, even to a point horrifically worse than Hiroshima or Nagasaki.

The world's reigning power accords itself the right to wage war at will, under a doctrine of "anticipatory self-defense" that covers any contingency it chooses. The means of destruction are to be unlimited.

U.S. military expenditures approximate those of the rest of the world combined, while arms sales by thirty-eight North American companies (one in Canada) account for over 60 percent of the world total (which rose 25 percent since 2002).

There have been efforts to strengthen the thin thread on which survival hangs. The most important is the Nuclear Non-

Proliferation Treaty (NPT), which came into force in 1970. The regular five-year review conference of the NPT took place at the United Nations in May (2005).

The NPT has been facing collapse, primarily because of the failure of the nuclear states to live up to their obligation under Article VI to pursue "good faith" efforts to eliminate nuclear weapons. The United States has led the way in refusal to abide by the Article VI obligations. Mohamed ElBaradei, head of the International Atomic Energy Agency, emphasizes that "reluctance by one party to fulfill its obligations breeds reluctance in others."

Ex-president Jimmy Carter blasted the United States as

> the major culprit in this erosion of the NPT. While claiming to be protecting the world from proliferation threats in Iraq, Libya, Iran and North Korea, American leaders not only have abandoned existing treaty restraints but also have asserted plans to test and develop new weapons, including antiballistic missiles, the earth-penetrating "bunker buster" and perhaps some new 'small' bombs. They also have abandoned past pledges and now threaten first use of nuclear weapons against non-nuclear states.

The thread has almost snapped in the years since Hiroshima, repeatedly. The best-known case was the Cuban Missile Crisis of October 1962, "the most dangerous moment in human history," as Arthur Schlesinger, historian and former adviser to President John F. Kennedy, observed in October 2002 at a retrospective conference in Havana.

The world "came within a hair's breadth of nuclear disaster," recalls Robert McNamara, Kennedy's defense secretary, who also attended the retrospective. In the May-June (2005) issue of *Foreign Policy*, he accompanies this reminder with a renewed warning of "apocalypse soon."

McNamara regards "current U.S. nuclear weapons policy as immoral, illegal, militarily unnecessary and dreadfully dangerous," creating "unacceptable risks to other nations and to our own," both the risk of "accidental or inadvertent nuclear launch," which is "unacceptably high," and of nuclear attack by terrorists. McNamara endorses the judgment of William Perry, President Bill Clinton's defense secretary, that "there is a greater than 50 percent probability of a nuclear strike on U.S. targets within a decade."

Similar judgments are commonly expressed by prominent strategic analysts. In his book *Nuclear Terrorism* (2004), Harvard international relations specialist Graham Allison reports the "consensus in the national security community" (of which he has been a part) that a "dirty bomb" attack is "inevitable," and an attack with a nuclear weapon highly likely, if fissionable materials—the essential ingredient—are not retrieved and secured. Allison reviews the partial success of efforts to do so since the early 1990s, under the initiatives of Senator Sam Nunn and Senator Richard Lugar, and the setback to these programs from the first days of the Bush administration, paralyzed by what Senator Joseph Biden called "ideological idiocy."

The Washington leadership has put aside nonproliferation programs and devoted its energies and resources to driving the country to war by deceit, then trying to manage the catastrophe it created in Iraq. The threat and use of violence is stimulating nuclear proliferation along with jihadi terrorism.

A high-level review of the "war on terror" two years after the invasion "focused on how to deal with the rise of a new generation of terrorists, schooled in Iraq over the past couple years,"

Susan B. Glasser reports in the *Washington Post*. "Top government officials are increasingly turning their attention to anticipate what one called 'the bleed out' of hundreds or thousands of Iraq-trained jihadists back to their home countries throughout the Middle East and Western Europe. 'It's a new piece of a new equation,' a former senior Bush administration official said. 'If you don't know who they are in Iraq, how are you going to locate them in Istanbul or London?'"

U.S. terrorism specialist Peter Bergen says in the *Boston Globe* that "the president is right that Iraq is a main front in the war on terrorism, but this is a front we created."

Shortly after the London bombing, Chatham House, Britain's premier foreign affairs institution, released a study drawing the obvious conclusion—denied with outrage by the government—that "the UK is at particular risk because it is the closest ally of the United States, has deployed armed forces in the military campaigns to topple the Taliban regime in Afghanistan and in Iraq . . . [and is] a pillion passenger" of American policy, sitting behind the driver of the motorcycle.

The probability of apocalypse soon cannot be realistically estimated, but it is surely too high for any sane person to contemplate with equanimity. While speculation is pointless, reaction to the threat of another Hiroshima is definitely not. On the contrary, it is urgent, particularly in the United States, because of Washington's primary role in accelerating the race to destruction by extending its historically unique military dominance coupled with policies of aggressive militarism, both in word and in deed, that are virtually an invitation to disaster.

9/11 and the Doctrine of Good Intentions

AUGUST 30, 2005

It is no easy task to gain some understanding of human affairs. In some respects, it is harder than the natural sciences. Mother Nature doesn't readily provide the answers, but at least she doesn't go out of her way to set up barriers to understanding.

In human affairs, it is necessary to detect and dismantle barriers erected by doctrinal systems, which adopt a range of devices that flow very naturally from concentration of power. Sometimes that is frankly acknowledged: for example, by Harvard Professor of the Science of Government, Samuel Huntingon, who explained the function of the Soviet threat in 1981, just as the incoming Reagan administration was cranking up the Cold War. "You may have to sell [intervention or other military action] in such a way as to create the misimpression that it is the Soviet Union that you are fighting," he wrote. "That is what the United States has done ever since the Truman Doctrine."

To facilitate the marketing effort, doctrinal systems commonly portray the current enemy as diabolical by its very nature. The characterization is sometimes accurate, but the crimes are rarely the source of the call for forceful measures against some target that stands in the way of current plans.

A recent illustration is Saddam Hussein—a defenseless target characterized as an awesome threat to our survival, who was linked to 9/11, and about to attack us again.

In 1982, the Reagan administration dropped Saddam's Iraq from the list of states supporting terrorism so that the flow of military and other aid to the murderous tyrant could begin. It continued long after Saddam's worst atrocities and the end of his war with Iran, and included means to develop weapons of mass destruction. The record, hardly obscure, falls under the "general tacit agreement that 'it wouldn't do' to mention that particular fact," in Orwell's phrase.

It is necessary to create misimpressions not only about the current "Great Satans" but also about one's own unique nobility. In particular, aggression and terror must be portrayed as self-defense and dedication to inspiring visions.

Emperor Hirohito of Japan, in his surrender declaration in August 1945, told his people, "We declared war on America and Britain out of our sincere desire to ensure Japan's self-preservation and the stabilization of East Asia, it being far from our thought either to infringe upon the sovereignty of other nations or to embark upon territorial aggrandizement."

The history of international crimes overflows with similar sentiments, including the lowest depths. Writing in 1935, with the dark clouds of Nazism settling, Martin Heidegger declared that Germany must now forestall "the peril of world darkening" beyond the nation's borders. With its "new spiritual energies" revived under Nazi rule, Germany is at last able "to take on its historic mission" of saving the world from "annihilation" by the "indifferent mass" elsewhere, primarily America and Russia.

Even individuals of the highest intelligence and moral integrity succumb to the pathology. At the peak of Britain's crimes in India and China, of which he had an intimate knowledge, John Stuart Mill wrote his classic essay on humanitarian intervention, urging Britain to undertake the enterprise vigorously—even though it will be "held up to obloquy" by backward Europeans who can't comprehend that England is "a novelty in the world," a nation that acts only "in the service of others," selflessly bearing the costs of bringing peace and justice to the world.

The image of righteous exceptionalism appears to be close to universal. For the United States, one constant theme is the dedication to bring democracy and independence to a suffering world.

The standard story in scholarship and in the media is that U.S. foreign policy oscillates between two conflicting tendencies. One is what is called Wilsonian idealism, which is based on noble intentions. The other is sober realism, which says that we have to realize the limitations of our good intentions. Those are the only two options.

Whatever the operative rhetoric, it takes discipline not to recognize the elements of truth in historian Arno Mayer's observation that since 1947, America has been a major perpetrator of "state terror" and other "'rogue' actions," causing immense harm, "always in the name of democracy, liberty and justice."

For the United States the longtime enemy has been independent nationalism, particularly when it threatens to become a "virus" that might spread contagion, to borrow Henry Kissinger's reference to democratic socialism in Chile after Salvador Allende was elected president in 1970. The virus therefore had to be extirpated, as it was, on September 11, 1973, a date often called "the first 9/11" in Latin America.

On that date, after years of U.S. subversion, General Augusto Pinochet's forces attacked the Chilean presidential palace. Allende died, an apparent suicide, unwilling to surrender to the assault that demolished Latin America's oldest and most vibrant democracy, and Pinochet established a brutal regime. The official death toll of the first 9/11 is 3,200; the actual toll is commonly estimated at about double that figure. In per capita terms, that would amount to 50,000–100,000 killed in the United States. Victims of hideous torture were later estimated at 30,000; that would be 700,000 people in the U.S., in per capita equivalent.

Washington firmly supported Pinochet's regime and had no slight role in its initial triumph. Pinochet soon moved to integrate other U.S.-backed Latin American military dictatorships in the international state terrorist network, "Operation Condor," that wreaked havoc in Latin America.

This is one of all-too-many similar illustrations of "democracy promotion" in the hemisphere and elsewhere.

Now we are instructed to believe that the U.S. mission in Afghanistan and Iraq is to bring democracy there.

"Muslims do not 'hate our freedom,' but rather they hate our policies," concludes a report last September (2004) by the Defense Science Board (DSB), a Pentagon advisory panel, adding that "when American public diplomacy talks about bringing democracy to Islamic societies, this is seen as no more than self-serving hypocrisy." As Muslims see it, the report continues, "American occupation of Afghanistan and Iraq has not led to democracy there, but only to more chaos and suffering."

In a *Financial Times* article in July (2005), citing the DSB report, David Gardner observes: "For the most part, Arabs plausibly believe it was Osama bin Laden who smashed the status quo, not George W. Bush, (because) the 9/11 attacks made it impossible for the West and its Arab despot clients to continue to ignore a political set-up that incubated blind rage against them"—a judgment that may prove too optimistic.

It should come as no surprise that the United States is very much like other powerful states, past and present, pursuing strategic and economic interests of dominant sectors to the accompaniment of rhetorical flourishes about its exceptional dedication to the highest value.

Against the backdrop of the disaster unfolding in Iraq, an uncritical faith in good intentions only delays a desperately needed redress of approach and policy.

The Bush Administration during Hurricane Season

SEPTEMBER 30, 2005

As the survivors of Hurricane Katrina try to piece their lives back together, it is all the clearer that a long-gathering storm of misguided policies and priorities preceded the tragedy.

In a pre-9/11 report, the Federal Emergency Management Agency (FEMA) had listed a major hurricane in New Orleans as one of the three most likely catastrophes to strike the United States. The others: a terrorist attack in New York and an earthquake in San Francisco.

New Orleans had become an urgent priority at FEMA since January (2005), when the agency's now-departed director Michael Brown returned from touring the tsunami devastation in Asia. "New Orleans was the No. 1 disaster we were talking about," Eric L. Tolbert, a former FEMA official, told the *New York Times*. "We were obsessed with New Orleans because of the risk." A year before Katrina hit, FEMA conducted a successful simulated-hurricane drill for New Orleans, but FEMA's elaborate plans were not implemented.

The war played a role in the failure. National Guard troops that had been sent to Iraq "took a lot of needed equipment with them, including dozens of high-water vehicles, Humvees, refueling tankers and generators that would be needed in the event a major natural disaster hit the state," the *Wall Street Journal* reported. "A senior Army official said the service was reluctant to commit the 4th brigade of the 10th Mountain Division from Fort Polk, because the unit, which numbers several thousand soldiers, is in the midst of preparing for an Afghanistan deployment."

Bureaucratic maneuvering also trumped the risk of natural disaster. Former FEMA officials told the *Chicago Tribune* that the agency's capabilities were "effectively marginalized" under President George W. Bush when the agency was folded into the Homeland Security Department, with fewer resources and extra layers of bureaucracy, a "brain drain" as demoralized employees left, and a completely unqualified Bush political crony put in charge. Once a "tier-one federal agency," FEMA now isn't "even in the back seat," Eric Holdeman, director of emergency management in King County, Washington, told the *Financial Times*. "They are in the trunk of the Department of Homeland Security car."

Bush funding cuts in 2004 compelled the Army Corps of Engineers to reduce flood-control work sharply, including badly needed strengthening of the levees that protected New Orleans. Bush's 2005 budget called for another serious reduction—a specialty of Bush-administration timing, much like the proposed sharp cut in security for public transportation right before bombings in London's public transport system in July 2005.

Disregard for the environment was another factor in this perfect storm. Wetlands help reduce the power of hurricanes and storm surges, but Sandra Postel, a water-policy expert, wrote in the *Christian Science Monitor* that wetlands were "largely missing when Katrina struck," in part because "the Bush administration in 2003 effectively gutted the 'no net loss' of wetlands policy initiated during the administration of the elder Bush."

The human toll of Katrina is incalculable, especially among the region's poorest citizens, but a relevant number is the 28 percent poverty rate in New Orleans—more than twice the national rate. During the Bush administration the U.S. poverty rate has grown, and welfare's limited safety net has been weakened further. The effects were so striking that even the right-wing media were appalled by the scale of the class-based and race-based devastation.

While the media were showing vivid scenes of human misery, the back pages reported that Republican leaders wasted no time in "using relief measures for the hurricane-ravaged Gulf coast to achieve a broad range of conservative economic and social policies," the *Wall Street Journal* reported.

Those agenda-promoting measures include suspending rules that require payment of prevailing wages by federal contractors and providing displaced schoolchildren with vouchers—another underhanded blow at the public-school system. They included lifting environmental restrictions, "waiving the estate tax for deaths in the storm-affected states"—a great boon for the population fleeing New Orleans slums—and in general making it clear once again that cynicism knows few bounds.

Lost in the flood is a concern for the needs of cities and for human services. The larger agenda of enhancing global domination and domestic concentrations of wealth and power takes precedence.

The images of suffering in Iraq, and in the aftermath of Hurricane Katrina, could hardly depict the consequences more vividly.

"Intelligent Design" and Its Consequences

NOVEMBER 2, 2005

President George W. Bush favors teaching both evolution and "intelligent design" in schools, "so people can know what the debate is about."

To proponents, intelligent design is the notion that the universe is too complex to have developed without a nudge from a power higher than evolution or natural selection. To detractors, intelligent design is creationism—the literal interpretation of the book of Genesis—in a thin guise, or simply vacuous, about as interesting as "I don't understand," as has always been true in the sciences before understanding is reached. Accordingly, there cannot be a "debate."

The teaching of evolution has long been difficult in the United States. Now a national movement has emerged to promote the teaching of intelligent design in schools. The issue has famously surfaced in a courtroom in Dover, Pennsylvania, where a school board is requiring students to hear a statement about intelligent design in a biology class—and parents mindful of the U.S. Constitution's church-state separation have sued the board.

In the interest of fairness, perhaps the president's speech-writers should take him seriously when they have him say that schools should be open-minded and teach all points of view. So far, however, the curriculum has not encompassed one obvious point of view: malignant design.

Unlike intelligent design, for which the evidence is zero, malignant design has tons of empirical evidence, much more than Darwinian evolution, by some criteria: the world's cruelty.

Be that as it may, the background of the current evolution–intelligent design controversy is the widespread rejection of science, a phenomenon with deep roots in American history that has been cynically exploited for narrow political gain during the last quarter century.

Intelligent design raises the question whether it is intelligent to disregard scientific evidence about matters of supreme importance to the nation and world—like global warming.

An old-fashioned conservative would believe in the value of Enlightenment ideals—rationality, critical analysis, freedom of speech, freedom of inquiry—and would try to adapt them to a modern society. The Founding Fathers, children of the Enlightenment, championed those ideals and took pains to create a constitution that espoused religious freedom yet took pains to separate church and state. The United States, despite the occasional messianism of its leaders, isn't a theocracy.

In our time, Bush administration hostility to scientific inquiry puts the world at risk. Environmental catastrophe, whether you think the world has been developing only since Genesis or for eons, is far too serious to ignore.

In preparation for the G8 summit this past summer (2005), the scientific academies of all G8 nations (including the U.S. National Academy of Sciences), joined by those of China, India, and Brazil, called on the leaders of the rich countries to take urgent action to head off global warming. "The scientific understanding of climate change is now sufficiently clear to justify prompt action," their statement said. "It is vital that all nations identify cost-effective steps that they can take now, to contribute to substantial and long-term reduction in net global greenhouse gas emissions."

In its lead editorial, the *Financial Times* endorsed this "clarion call," while observing: "There is, however, one holdout, and unfortunately it is to be found in the White House where . . . George W. Bush . . . insists we still do not know enough about this literally world-changing phenomenon."

Dismissal of scientific evidence on matters of survival, in keeping with Bush's scientific judgment, is routine. A few months earlier, at the 2005 annual meeting of the American Association for the Advancement of Science, leading U.S. climate researchers released "the most compelling evidence yet" that human activities are responsible for global warming, according to the *Financial Times*. They predicted major climatic effects, including severe reductions in water supplies in regions that rely on rivers fed by melting snow and glaciers.

Other prominent researchers at the same session reported evidence that the melting of Arctic and Greenland ice sheets is causing changes in the sea's salinity balance that threaten "to shut down the Ocean Conveyor Belt, which transfers heat from the tropics toward the polar regions through currents such as the Gulf Stream." Such changes might bring significant temperature reduction to northern Europe.

Like the statement of the national scientific academies for the G8 summit, the release of "the most compelling evidence yet" received scant notice in the United States, despite the attention given in the same days to the implementation of the Kyoto Protocol, with the most important government refusing to take part.

It is important to stress "government." The standard report that the United States stands almost alone in rejecting the Kyoto Protocol is correct only if the phrase "United States" excludes its population, which strongly favors the Kyoto pact (73 percent, according to a July [2005] poll by the Program on International Policy Attitudes).

Perhaps only the word "malignant" could describe a failure to acknowledge, much less address, the all-too-scientific issue of climate change. Thus the "moral clarity" of the Bush administration extends to its cavalier attitude toward the fate of our grandchildren.

South America at the Tipping Point

"How Venezuela Is Keeping the Home Fires Burning in Massachusetts," reads a recent full-page ad in major U.S. newspapers from PDVSA, Venezuela's state-owned oil company, and CITGO, its Houston-based subsidiary. The ad describes a program, encouraged by Venezuelan President Hugo Chávez, to sell heating oil at discount prices to low-income communities in Boston, the South Bronx, and elsewhere in the United States—one of the more ironic gestures ever in the North-South dialogue.

There is a background. The deal developed after a group of U.S. senators sent a letter to nine major oil companies asking them to donate a portion of their recent record profits to help poor residents cover heating bills. The only response came from CITGO.

In the United States, commentary on the deal is grudging at best, saying that Chávez, who has accused the Bush administration of trying to overthrow his government, is motivated by political ends—unlike, for example, the purely humanitarian programs of the U.S. Agency for International Development.

Chávez's heating oil is one among many challenges bubbling up from Latin America for the Washington planners of grand strategy. The noisy protests during President Bush's trip last month (November 2005) to the Summit of the Americas, in Argentina, illustrate the dilemma.

From Venezuela to Argentina, the hemisphere is falling out of control, with left-center governments almost all the way through. Even in Central America, still suffering the aftereffects of President Reagan's "war on terror," the lid is barely on.

In South America, the indigenous populations have become much more active and influential, particularly in Bolivia and Ecuador, both major energy producers, where they either oppose production of oil and gas or want it to be domestically controlled. Some are even calling for an "Indian nation" in South America.

Meanwhile internal economic integration is strengthening, reversing relative isolation that dates back to the Spanish conquests. Furthermore, South-South interaction is growing, with major powers (Brazil, South Africa, India) in the lead, particularly on economic issues. Latin America as a whole is increasing trade and other relations with the European Union and China, with some setbacks, but likely expansion, especially for raw materials exporters like Brazil and Chile. Venezuela has forged probably the closest relations with China of any Latin American country and is planning to sell increasing amounts of oil to China as part of its effort to reduce dependence on a hostile U.S. government.

Washington's thorniest problem in the region is Venezuela, which provides nearly 15 percent of U.S. oil imports. President Hugo Chávez, elected in 1998, displays the kind of independence that the United States translates as defiance—as with Chávez's ally Fidel Castro. In 2002, Washington embraced President Bush's vision of democracy by supporting a military coup that very briefly overturned the Chávez government. The Bush administration had to back down, however, because of opposition to the coup throughout Latin America, and the quick reversal of the coup by a popular uprising.

Compounding Washington's distress, Cuba and Venezuela are establishing closer relations. Joint Cuba-Venezuela projects are also having a considerable impact in the Caribbean countries, where, under a program called Operation Miracle, Cuban doctors are providing health care to people who had no hope of receiving it, with Venezuelan funding.

Chávez has repeatedly won monitored elections and referenda despite overwhelming and bitter media hostility. Support for the elected government has soared during the Chávez years.[1]

The veteran Latin American correspondent Hugh O'Shaughnessy explains why in a report for *Irish Times*:

> In Venezuela, where an oil economy has over the decades produced a sparkling elite of superrich, a quarter of under-15s go hungry, for instance, and 60 per cent of people over 59 have no income at all. Less than a fifth of the population enjoys social security. Only now under President Chavez . . . has medicine started to become something of a reality for the poverty-stricken majority in the rich but deeply divided—virtually nonfunctioning—society. Since he won power in democratic elections and began to transform the health and welfare sector which catered so badly to the mass of the population progress has been slow. But it has been perceptible . . .

Now Venezuela is joining MERCOSUR, South America's leading trade bloc. MERCOSUR, which already includes Argentina, Brazil, Paraguay and Uruguay, presents an alternative to the so-called Free Trade Agreement of the Americas, backed by the United States.

At issue in the region, as elsewhere around the world, are alternative social and economic models. Enormous, unprecedented popular movements have developed to expand cross-border integration—going beyond economic agendas to encompass human rights, environmental concerns, cultural independence, and people-to-people contacts. These movements are ludicrously called "anti-globalization" because they favor globalization directed to the interests of people, not investors and financial institutions.

U.S. problems in the Americas extend north as well as south. For obvious reasons, Washington has hoped to rely more on Canada, Venezuela, and other non–Middle East oil resources. But Canada's relations with the United States are more "strained and combative" than ever before as a result of, among other issues, Washington's rejection of NAFTA decisions favoring Canada. As Joel Brinkley reports in the *New York Times*, "Partly as a result, Canada is working hard to build up its relationship with China [and] some officials are saying Canada may shift a significant portion of its trade, particularly oil, from the United States to China."

It takes real talent for Washington to alienate even Canada.

Washington's Latin American policies are further enhancing U.S. isolation. One recent example: For the fourteenth year in a row, the UN General Assembly voted against the U.S. embargo against Cuba. The vote on the resolution was 182 to 4: the United States, Israel, the Marshall Islands, and Palau. Micronesia abstained. In reality, then, 182 to 1.[2]

NOTES

1. A December 2006 report by the respected Chilean polling organization Latinobarómetro found that Venezuela ranked

a close second to Uruguay (or tied with it) in positive evalua-
tion of democracy in the country, choice of democracy as best
form of government, and judging elections the most effective
way to change things. It ranked highest in judging that the
government works for benefit of all, not a few powerful
groups; and in evaluating the country's economic situation,
prospects for the future, and the government's economic policies. It was one of five countries in which a majority says
elections are clean. The poll was mentioned in the U.S. media
when president Bush set off to Latin America with "a marked
shift in Washington's priorities for Latin America aimed at
countering the challenge posed by President Hugo Chávez of
Venezuela" (Larry Rohter, "Bush to Set Out Shift in Agenda
on Latin Trip," *New York Times*, March 6, 2007.) The meaning
of the fact that Bush is "countering Chávez" by trying to
mimic his rhetoric (though not the programs, beyond a pit-
tance) did not seem to register. But the poll was indeed
mentioned, at last, in this connection: namely, its finding that
outside of Venezuela, Chávez's negative ratings are similar to
Bush's (John McKinnon and Matt Moffett, "Bush Poised to
Counter Chávez," *Wall Street Journal*, March 5, 2007, and Sara
Miller-Lana and Mark Rice-Oxley, "Chávez's Oil Largesse
Winning Fans Abroad," *Christian Science Monitor*, March 5,
2007). These are the only references to the poll I have seen in
the press, which regularly echoes and amplifies Washington
oratory about the destruction of democracy in Venezuela. All
of this, however, scarcely reaches the level of the constant
drumbeat of hysterical propaganda about Chávez in the dominant right-wing media in much of Latin America, an
interesting topic for more careful inquiry.
2. In November 2006, the vote changed to 183 to 4—the same
   four.

The Hidden Meaning of the Iraqi Elections

JANUARY 4, 2006

President Bush called last month's (December 2005) Iraqi elections a "major milestone in the march to democracy." They are indeed a milestone—just not the kind that Washington would welcome.

Disregarding the standard declarations of benign intent on the part of leaders, let's review the history. When Bush and Britain's prime minister, Tony Blair, invaded Iraq, the pretext, insistently repeated, was a "single question": Will Iraq eliminate its weapons of mass destruction? Within a few months this "single question" was answered the wrong way. Then, very quickly, the real reason for the invasion became Bush's "messianic mission" to bring democracy to Iraq and the Middle East.

Even apart from the timing, the democratization bandwagon runs up against the fact that the United States has tried, in every possible way, to prevent elections in Iraq. Last January's (2005) elections came about because of mass nonviolent resistance which U.S. forces could not contain. Few competent observers would disagree with the editors of the *Financial Times*, who wrote last March (2005) that "the reason [the elections] took place was the insistence of the Grand Ayatollah Ali Sistani, who vetoed three schemes by the U.S.-led occupation authorities to shelve or dilute them."

Elections, if taken seriously, mean you pay some attention to the will of the population. The crucial question for an invading army is: Do they want us to be here?

There is no lack of information about the answer. One important source is a poll for the British Ministry of Defense this past August (2005), carried out by Iraqi university researchers and leaked to the British press. It found that 82 percent are "strongly opposed" to the presence of coalition troops and less than 1 percent believe they are responsible for any improvement in security.

Analysts of the Brookings Institution in Washington report that in November (2005), 80 percent of Iraqis favored "near-term U.S. troop withdrawal." Other sources generally concur.[1]

So the coalition forces should withdraw, as the population wants them to, instead of trying desperately to set up a client regime with military forces that they can control.

But Bush and Blair still refuse to set a timetable for withdrawal, so far limiting themselves to possible token withdrawals as their goals are achieved.

There's a good reason why the United States cannot tolerate a sovereign, more or less democratic Iraq. The issue can scarcely be raised because it conflicts with firmly established doctrine: We're supposed to believe that the United States would have invaded Iraq if it were an island in the Indian Ocean and its main export were pickles, not petroleum.

As is obvious to anyone not committed to the party line, taking control of Iraq will enormously strengthen U.S. power over global energy resources, a crucial lever of world control.

Suppose that Iraq were to become sovereign and democratic. Imagine the policies it would be likely to pursue. The Shiite population in the south, where most of Iraq's oil is, would have a predominant influence. They would prefer friendly relations with Shiite Iran. The relations are already close. The Badr Brigade, the militia that largely controls the south, was trained in Iran. The highly influential clerics also have long-standing relations with Iran, including Ayatollah Sistani, who grew up there. And the Shiite-dominant interim government has already begun to establish economic and possibly military relations with Iran.

Furthermore, right across the border in Saudi Arabia is a substantial, bitterly oppressed Shiite population. Any move toward independence in Iraq is likely to increase efforts to gain a degree of autonomy and justice there, too. This also happens to be the region where most of Saudi Arabia's oil is.

The outcome could be a loose Shiite alliance comprising Iraq, Iran, and the major oil regions of Saudi Arabia, independent of Washington and controlling large portions of the world's oil reserves.

It's not unlikely that an independent bloc of this kind might follow Iran's lead in developing major energy projects jointly with China and India.

Iran may give up on western Europe, assuming that it will be unwilling to act independently of the United States. China, however, can't be intimidated. That's why the United States is so frightened by China.

China is already establishing relations with Iran—and even with Saudi Arabia, both military and economic. There is an Asian energy security grid, based on China and Russia, but probably bringing in India, Korea, and others. If Iran moves in that direction, it can become the linchpin of that power grid.

Such developments, including a sovereign Iraq and possibly even major Saudi energy resources, would be the ultimate nightmare for Washington.

Also, the labor movement is re-establishing itself in Iraq, a very important development. Washington insists on keeping Saddam Hussein's bitter antilabor laws, but the labor movement continues its organizing work despite these laws and very harsh conditions. Their activists are being killed. Nobody knows by whom, maybe by insurgents, maybe by former Baathists, maybe by somebody else. But they're persisting. They constitute one of the major democratizing forces that have deep roots in Iraqi history and that might revitalize, also much to the horror of the occupying forces.

One critical question is how Westerners will react. Will we be on the side of the occupying forces trying to prevent democracy and sovereignty? Or will we be on the side of the Iraqi people?

NOTES

1. Mid-2006 polls by the State Department and Program on International Policy Attitudes found that two-thirds of Baghdadis want U.S. forces to leave immediately, and large majorities favored withdrawal within a year or less. Eighty percent think that presence of U.S. forces increases violence, and 60 percent regard attacks on U.S. forces as legitimate. The figures are much higher in Arab Iraq, where troops are actually deployed. The figures have been steadily rising.

The Hamas Victory and "Democracy Promotion"

FEBRUARY 9, 2006

Hamas's electoral victory is ominous but unfortunately understandable, in light of recent developments.

It is fair to describe Hamas as radical, extremist, violent, and as a threat to peace and a just political settlement. But it is useful to remember that in crucial respects Hamas is not as extremist as the U.S. and Israel. For example, Hamas states that it will agree to a long-term truce on the internationally recognized pre–June 1967 border, while pursuing negotiations on a political settlement. The idea is completely foreign to the United States and Israel, which reject any restrictions on their resort to violence, refuse to negotiate, and insist that any political outcome must include Israeli takeover of substantial parts of the West Bank (and perhaps the forgotten Golan Heights).

Hamas won by combining strong resistance to military occupation with grassroots social organizing and service to the poor—a platform and practice likely to win votes anywhere.

For the Bush administration, however, the victory presents yet another obstacle in its policy of deterring democracy, officially called "democracy promotion" in reigning Newspeak.

Washington's stance toward elections in Palestine has been consistent. Elections were on hold until the death of Yasser Arafat, because it was taken for granted that he would win. Uncontroversially, elections cannot be permitted if the wrong candidate might win. Arafat's death was hailed as an opportunity for the realization of Bush's "vision" of a democratic Palestinian state—a pale and vague reflection of the international consensus on a two-state settlement that the United States has blocked for thirty years.

In an analysis in the *New York Times* just after Arafat's death, "Hoping Democracy Can Replace a Palestinian Icon," Steven Erlanger opens by explaining that "The post-Arafat era will be the latest test of a quintessentially American article of faith: that elections provide legitimacy even to the frailest institutions."

In the final paragraph we read: "The paradox for the Palestinians is rich, however. In the past, the Bush administration resisted new national elections among the Palestinians. The thought then was that the elections would make Mr. Arafat look better and give him a fresher mandate, and might help give credibility and authority to Hamas."

In brief, the "quintessential article of faith" is that elections are fine, as long as they come out the right way.

The problem has a recent counterpart. In Iraq, mass nonviolent resistance compelled Washington and London to permit the elections they had sought to block by a series of schemes. The subsequent effort to subvert the unwanted elections by providing substantial advantages to the administration's favorite candidate, and expelling the independent media, also failed.

Washington resorted to the standard modes of subversion in Palestine, too. Last month (January 2006) the *Washington Post* reported that the U.S. Agency for International Development became an "invisible conduit" in an effort to "increase the popularity of the Palestinian Authority on the eve of crucial elections in which the governing party faces a serious challenge from the radical Islamic group Hamas." And the *New York Times* reported: "The United States spent about $1.9 million of its yearly $400 million in aid to the Palestinians on dozens of quick projects before elections this week to bolster the governing Fatah faction's image with voters and strengthen its hand in competing with the militant faction Hamas."

As is normal, the U.S. consulate in East Jerusalem assured the press that the concealed efforts to promote Fatah were merely intended "to enhance democratic institutions and support democratic actors, not just Fatah."

In the United States or any Western country, even a hint of such foreign interference would destroy a candidate, but deeply rooted imperial mentality legitimates such routine measures of subversion of elections elsewhere. However, the attempt again resoundingly failed.

The U.S. and Israeli governments now have to adjust to dealing somehow with a radical Islamic party that approaches their own traditional rejection of the international consensus, though not entirely, at least if Hamas really means to agree to a truce on the pre-1967 border.

Hamas's formal commitment to "destroy Israel" places it on a par with the United States and Israel, which vowed formally that there could be no "additional Palestinian state" (in addition to Jordan) until they relaxed their extreme rejectionist stand partially in the past few years, agreeing to a "statelet" of fragments that remain after Israeli takeover of what it wants in Palestine.

For the sake of argument, imagine a reversal of circumstances—Hamas's agreeing to allow Israelis to remain in scattered, unviable cantons, virtually separated from one another and from some small part of Jerusalem, while Palestine constructs huge settlement and infrastructure projects to take over the valuable land and resources and make travel virtually impossible for Israelis, even for ambulances. And Hamas's agreeing to call the fragments "a state."

If proposals for this impoverished form of "statehood" were made, we would—rightly—be horrified, perhaps warning of a revival of Nazism and calling for charges against Hamas at the World Court for inciting genocide, in violation of the Genocide Convention. But with such proposals, Hamas's position would be essentially like that of the United States and Israel.

NOTES

A few days after this article appeared, U.S. elites (joined by Europe) provided a dramatic demonstration of their visceral hatred of democracy (unless it turns out as they wish—the "strong line of continuity" found by Thomas Carothers). They decided to support Israel's program of extremely harsh punishment of Palestinians for voting "the wrong way" in a free election. As is normal, elite opinion could not detect what this clearly entails. For more on the matter, see Gilbert Achcar, Noam Chomsky, and Stephen Shalom, *Perilous Power* (2007).

Asia, the Americas, and the Reigning Superpower

MARCH 7, 2006

The prospect that Europe and Asia might move toward greater independence has troubled U.S. planners since World War II. The concerns have only risen as the "tripolar order"—Europe, North America and Asia—has continued to evolve.

Every day, Latin America, too, is becoming more independent. Now Asia and the Americas are strengthening their ties while the reigning superpower, the odd man out, consumes itself in misadventures in the Middle East.

Regional integration in Asia and Latin America is a crucial and increasingly important issue that, from Washington's perspective, betokens a defiant world falling out of control. Energy, of course, remains a defining factor—the object of contention—everywhere.

China, unlike Europe, refuses to be intimidated by Washington, a primary reason for the fear of China by U.S planners. That presents a dilemma: Steps toward confrontation are inhibited by U.S. corporate reliance on China as an export platform and growing market, as well as China's financial reserves, reported to be approaching Japan's in scale.

In January (2006), Saudi Arabia's King Abdullah visited Beijing, which is expected to lead to a Sino-Saudi memorandum of understanding calling for "increased cooperation and investment between the two countries in oil, natural gas and minerals," the *Wall Street Journal* reports.

Already much of Iran's oil goes to China, and China is providing Iran with weapons that both states presumably regard as deterrent to U.S. designs.

India also has options. India may choose to be a U.S. client, or it may prefer to join the more independent Asian bloc that is taking shape, with ever more ties to Middle East oil producers. Siddarth Varadarajan, deputy editor of the *Hindu*, observes that "if the 21st century is to be an 'Asian century,' Asia's passivity in the energy sector has to end."

The key is India-China cooperation. In January (2006), an agreement signed in Beijing "cleared the way for India and China to collaborate not only in technology but also in hydrocarbon exploration and production, a partnership that could eventually alter fundamental equations in the world's oil and natural gas sector," Varadarajan points out.

An additional step, already being contemplated, is an Asian oil market trading in euros. The impact on the international financial system and the balance of global power could be significant.

It should be no surprise that President Bush paid a recent visit to try to keep India in the fold, offering nuclear cooperation and other inducements as a lure.[1]

Meanwhile, in Latin America, left-center governments prevail from Venezuela to Argentina. The indigenous populations have become much more active and influential, particularly in Bolivia and Ecuador, where they either want oil and gas to be domestically controlled or, in some cases, oppose production altogether. Many indigenous people apparently do not see any reason why their lives, societies, and cultures should be disrupted or destroyed so that New Yorkers can sit in their SUVs in traffic gridlock.

Venezuela, the leading oil exporter in the hemisphere, has forged probably the closest relations with China of any Latin American country and is planning to sell increasing amounts of oil to China as part of its effort to reduce dependence on the openly hostile U.S. government.

Venezuela has joined MERCOSUR, the South American customs union, a move described by Argentine President Nestor Kirchner as "a milestone" in the development of this trading bloc, and welcomed as a "new chapter in our integration" by Brazilian President Luiz Inácio Lula da Silva.

Venezuela, apart from supplying Argentina with fuel oil, bought almost a third of Argentine debt issued in 2005, one element of a regionwide effort to free the countries from the controls of the International Monetary Fund after two decades of disastrous conformity to the rules imposed by the U.S.-dominated international financial institutions.

Steps toward South American integration advanced further in December 2005 with the election of Evo Morales in Bolivia, the country's first indigenous president. Morales moved quickly to reach a series of energy accords with Venezuela. The *Financial Times* reported that these "are expected to underpin forthcoming radical reforms to Bolivia's economy and energy sector" with its huge gas reserves, second only to Venezuela's in South America.

Cuba-Venezuela relations are becoming ever closer, each relying on its comparative advantage. Venezuela is providing low-cost oil while in return Cuba organizes literacy and health programs, sending thousands of highly skilled professionals, teachers, and doctors, who work in the poorest and most neglected areas, as they do elsewhere in the Third World.

Cuban medical assistance is also being welcomed elsewhere. One of the most horrendous tragedies of recent years was the earthquake in Pakistan last October (2005). Besides the huge death toll, unknown numbers of survivors had to face brutal winter weather with little shelter, food, or medical assistance.

"Cuba has provided the largest contingent of doctors and paramedics to Pakistan," paying all the costs (perhaps with Venezuelan funding), writes John Cherian in India's *Frontline*, citing *Dawn*, a leading Pakistan daily. President Pervez Musharraf of Pakistan expressed his "deep gratitude" to Fidel Castro for the "spirit and compassion" of the Cuban medical teams— reported to comprise more than 1,000 trained personnel, 44 percent of them women, who remained to work in remote mountain villages, "living in tents in freezing weather and in an alien culture" after Western aid teams had been withdrawn.

Growing popular movements, primarily in the South but with increasing participation in the rich industrial countries, are serving as the bases for many of these developments toward more independence and concern for the needs of the great majority of the population.

NOTES

1. On December 18, 2006, after receiving overwhelming congressional approval, President Bush signed the United States-India Peaceful Atomic Energy Cooperation Act. As is a common practice, becoming routine since the Reagan-Gingrich years, the titles of acts of Congress are drawn from Orwell. This is no exception. The major thrust of the act is effective authorization of India's development of nuclear weapons outside the bounds of the Nuclear Non-Proliferation Treaty. It also offers India assistance in nuclear programs along with other rewards. The Bush initiative was unilateral (as usual), nuclear weapons specialist Gary Mil-

hollin reports, without the required notification or coordination with the international institutions (the Nuclear Suppliers Group, Missile Technology Control Regime) that had been established to stop the spread of nuclear weapons and delivery systems. The U.S.-India agreement violates the "cardinal principle of both regimes": that they are "country neutral." Washington "has invited other members to act the same way," Milhollin observes, perhaps by undertaking "unilateral deals with Iran or Pakistan" or others of their choice. Washington's new initiatives to undermine the barriers against nuclear war, he adds, "may hasten the day when a nuclear explosion destroys a U.S. city." The reasons, as Secretary of State Rice conceded, were to facilitate exports by U.S. firms. The primary interest, Milhollin suggests, is military aircraft. The message is that "export controls are less important to the United States than money"—that is, profits for U.S. corporations (*Current History*, November 2006). Shortly after, it was reported that China and India were about to sign a similar deal, which would give India "access to high-tech nuclear technology it was denied previously." The deal would enable India to "become equidistant between the U.S. and China," an Indian official explained, while in Chinese eyes, helping to develop Russia-China-India cooperation to balance U.S. global hegemony (Jehangir Pocha, "China and India on verge of nuclear deal," *Boston Globe*, November 20, 2006). Meanwhile Indian Prime Minister Manmohan Singh informed Parliament that "there is no question of allowing American inspectors to roam around our nuclear facilities," and foreign minister Pranab Mukerjee added that "We will not allow external scrutiny of or interference with the strategic program," meaning nuclear weapons development and testing (Pallava Bagla, "Indo-U.S. Nuclear Pact in Jeopardy," *Science*, 22 December 2006.)

The seriousness of these moves is underscored by Michael Krepon, cofounder of the Henry J. Stimson Center and a leading specialist on nuclear threat reduction. "Now that the United States has given India a free pass around nuclear controls," he writes, "other states will be lining up to profit from proliferation." The unilateral U.S. move to exempt India from the global rules of nuclear commerce has "no precedent," and if the other "primary potential profit-takers" in the Nuclear Suppliers Group— the five permanent members of the Security Council—follow the U.S. lead and "place profits ahead of nonproliferation," the nonproliferation regime will suffer yet another severe blow. "Simply put, as export controls go, so does the NPT," he concludes. "Senior Bush administration officials view the U.S.-India deal as a significant part of the administration's legacy," Krepon observes: "Unfortunately, they may be right." Krepon, "The Nuclear Flock," *Bulletin of the Atomic Scientists*, March/April 2007.

"Just War" Theory and the Real World

MAY 5, 2006

Spurred by these times of invasions and evasions, discussion of "just war" has had a renaissance among scholars and even among policymakers.

Meanwhile actions in the real world all too often reinforce the maxim of Thucydides that "the strong do as they can, while the weak suffer what they must"—which is not only indisputably unjust, but at the present stage of human civilization, a literal threat to the survival of the species. In its application, the contemporary revival of just war theory conforms rather well to the maxim.

In his highly praised reflections on just war, Michael Walzer describes the invasion of Afghanistan as "a triumph of just war theory," standing alongside Kosovo as a "just war." He presents no argument, just assertion. In these two cases, as throughout, his arguments rely crucially on premises like "seems to me entirely justified," or "I believe" or "no doubt."

Facts are ignored, even the most obvious ones. Consider Afghanistan. As the bombing began in October 2001, President Bush warned Afghans that it would continue until they handed over people that the United States suspected of terrorism.

The word "suspected" is important. Eight months later, FBI head Robert S. Mueller III told editors and reporters at the *Washington Post* that after what must have been the most intense manhunt in history, "We think the masterminds of [the September 11 attacks] were in Afghanistan, high in the al-Qaida leadership. Plotters and others—the principals—came together in Germany and perhaps elsewhere."

What was still unclear in June 2002 could not have been known definitively the preceding October, though few doubted at once that it was true. Nor did I, for what it's worth, but surmise and evidence are two different things. It seems fair to say that the circumstances—and this barely touches on them—raise a question about whether bombing Afghans was a transparent example of "just war."

Much the same is true of the bombing of Serbia in 1999, as has been discussed extensively elsewhere. Specifically, it is uncontroversial that the large-scale killings and expulsions were not the reason for the bombing, as constantly claimed, but its consequence, in fact its anticipated consequence, contrary to standard reversal of timing in media and sometimes scholarship.[1]

Walzer's charges—not arguments—are directed against unnamed targets (apart from unsupported slanders about Edward Said and Richard Falk)—for example, campus opponents who are "pacifists." He adds that their "pacifism" is a "bad argument," because he thinks violence is sometimes legitimate.

We may well agree that violence is sometimes legitimate (I do), but "I think" is hardly an overwhelming argument in the real-world cases that he discusses. Regrettably, this is not at all untypical of resort to "Just War theory" to justify Washington's resort to violence.[2]

By appeal to "just war," counterterrorism, or some other rationale, the United States exempts itself from the fundamental principles of world order that it played the primary role in formulating and enacting.

After World War II, a new regime of international law was instituted. Its provisions on laws of war are codified in the UN Charter, the Geneva Conventions, and the Nuremberg principles, adopted by the General Assembly. The UN Charter bars the threat or use of force unless authorized by the UN Security Council or, under Article 51, in self-defense against armed attack until the Security Council acts.

In 2004, a high-level UN panel, including, among others, former National Security Adviser Brent Scowcroft, concluded that

> Article 51 needs neither extension nor restriction of its long-understood scope . . .
>
> In a world full of perceived potential threats, the risk to the global order and the norm of nonintervention on which it continues to be based is simply too great for the legality of unilateral preventive action, as distinct from collectively endorsed action, to be accepted. Allowing one to so act is to allow all.

The National Security Strategy of September 2002, just largely reiterated in March (2006), grants the United States the right to carry out what it calls "pre-emptive war," which means not preemptive, but "preventive war" in direct violation of the UN Charter. That's the right to commit aggression, plain and simple.

The concept of aggression was defined clearly enough by U.S. Supreme Court Justice Robert Jackson, who was chief prosecutor for the United States at Nuremberg. The concept was restated in an authoritative UN General Assembly resolution. An "aggressor," Jackson proposed to the tribunal, is a state that is the first to commit such actions as "invasion of its armed forces, with or without a declaration of war, of the territory of another State."

Evidently, that applies to the invasion of Iraq.

Also pertinent are Justice Jackson's eloquent words at Nuremberg: "If certain acts of violation of treaties are crimes, they are crimes whether the United States does them or whether Germany does them, and we are not prepared to lay down a rule of criminal conduct against others which we would not be willing to have invoked against us." And elsewhere: "We must never forget that the record on which we judge these defendants is the record on which history will judge us tomorrow. To pass these defendants a poisoned chalice is to put it to our own lips as well."

For the political leadership, the threat of adherence to these principles—and to the rule of law in general—is serious indeed. Or it would be, if anyone dared to defy "the single ruthless superpower whose leadership intends to shape the world according to its own forceful world view," as military and political correspondent Reuven Pedatzur describes Washington in Israel's leading journal, *Haaretz*, last May (2005).

Let us bear in mind a few simple truths. The first is that actions are evaluated in terms of the range of plausibly anticipated consequences. A second is the principle of universality; we apply to ourselves the same standards we apply to others, if not more stringent ones.

Apart from being the merest truisms, these principles are also the foundation of just war theory, at least any version of it that deserves to be taken seriously. Not, unfortunately, the version that is presented by prominent advocates.

NOTES

1. See the review of extensive Western documentary evidence in my *A New Generation Draws the Line* (2000), updated since (see also *Hegemony or Survival* and *Failed States*). It has now been acknowledged at the highest level of the Clinton administration that the prime reason for the bombing was "not the plight of Kosovar Albanians"—as was obvious from overwhelming evidence right away—but rather "Yugoslavia's resistance to the broader trends of political and economic reform," code words for Washington's neoliberal programs. John Norris, *Collision Course* (2005).

   The foreword to *Collision Course* was written by John Norris's superior, Strobe Talbott, deputy secretary of state under Clinton with special responsibility for planning concerning the war. Talbott writes that "thanks to John Norris," those interested in the war in Kosovo "will know . . . how events looked and felt at the time to those of us who were involved" at the highest level.

   On Afghanistan, see "9/11 and the 'Age of Terror,'" note 1, page 38.

2. For discussion of moral philosopher Jean Bethke Elshtain's contributions, see *Hegemony or Survival*, chapter 8, and for more, the extended online edition.

Disarming the Iran Nuclear Showdown

JUNE 15, 2006

The urgency of halting the proliferation of nuclear weapons, and moving toward their elimination, could hardly be greater.

Failure to do so is very likely to lead to grim consequences, even the end of biology's only experiment with higher intelligence. As threatening as the crisis is, the means exist to defuse it.

A near meltdown seems to be imminent over Iran and its nuclear programs. Before 1979, when the shah of Iran was in power, Washington strongly supported these programs.

Today, the standard claim is that Iran has no need for nuclear power and, therefore, must be pursuing a secret weapons program. "For a major oil producer such as Iran, nuclear energy is a wasteful use of resources," Henry Kissinger wrote in the *Washington Post* last year (2005).

Thirty years ago, however, when Kissinger was secretary of state for President Gerald R. Ford, he held that "introduction of nuclear power will both provide for the growing needs of Iran's economy and free remaining oil reserves for export or conversion to petrochemicals."

Last year (2005), Dafna Linzer of the *Washington Post* asked Kissinger about his reversal of opinion. Kissinger responded with his usual engaging frankness: "They were an allied country"—so therefore they had a genuine need for nuclear energy.

In 1976, the Ford administration "endorsed Iranian plans to build a massive nuclear energy industry, but also worked hard to complete a multibillion-dollar deal that would have given Tehran control of large quantities of plutonium and enriched uranium—the two pathways to a nuclear bomb," Linzer wrote. The top planners of the Bush II administration, who are now denouncing these programs, were then in key national security posts: Dick Cheney, Donald Rumsfeld, and Paul Wolfowitz.

Iranians are surely not as willing as the West to discard history to the rubbish heap, including this chapter of history. They also know that the United States, along with its allies, has been tormenting Iranians for more than fifty years, ever since a U.S.-UK military coup overthrew the parliamentary government and installed the shah, who ruled with an iron hand until a popular uprising expelled him in 1979 while compiling an atrocious record of human rights violations, ignored by the media, which became deeply outraged over such violations after the U.S.-backed tyranny was overthrown.[1]

The Reagan administration then supported Saddam Hussein's invasion of Iran, providing him with military and other aid that helped him slaughter hundreds of thousands of Iranians (along with Iraqi Kurds). Then came President Clinton's harsh sanctions, followed by Bush's threats to attack Iran—themselves a serious breach of the UN Charter.

Last month (May 2006), the Bush administration conditionally agreed to join its European allies in direct talks with Iran; but it refused to withdraw the threat of attack, rendering virtually meaningless any negotiations offer that comes, in effect, at gunpoint. Recent history provides further reason for skepticism about Washington's intentions.

In May 2003, according to Flynt Leverett, then a senior official in Bush's National Security Council, the reformist government of Mohammad Khatami proposed "an agenda for a diplomatic process that was intended to resolve on a comprehensive basis all of the bilateral differences between the United States and Iran." Included were "weapons of mass destruction, a two-state solution to the Israeli-Palestinian conflict, the future of Lebanon's Hezbollah organization and cooperation with the UN nuclear safeguards agency," the *Financial Times* reported last month (May 2006). The Bush administration refused, and reprimanded the Swiss diplomat who conveyed the offer.[2]

A year later, the European Union and Iran struck a bargain: Iran would suspend uranium enrichment, and in return Europe would provide assurances that the United States and Israel would not attack Iran. Apparently under U.S. pressure, Europe backed off, and Iran renewed its enrichment processes.[3]

As in the case of the 2003 offers, and others, there is only one way to determine whether Iran's initiatives are serious: pursue them. From the record, we can only conclude that the U.S. and its allies are afraid that they might be serious.

The Iranian nuclear programs, as far as is known, fall within its rights under Article IV of the Nuclear Non-Proliferation Treaty, which grants non-nuclear states the right to produce fuel for nuclear energy. The Bush administration argues that Article IV should be strengthened, and I think that makes sense.

When the NPT came into force in 1970, there was a considerable gap between producing fuel for energy and for nuclear weapons. But advances in technology have narrowed the gap. However, any such revision of Article IV would have to ensure unimpeded access for nonmilitary use, in accord with the initial NPT bargain between declared nuclear powers and the non-nuclear states.

In 2003 a reasonable proposal to this end was put forth by Mohamed ElBaradei, head of the International Atomic Energy Agency: that all production and processing of weapon-usable material be under international control, with "assurance that legitimate would-be users could get their supplies." That should be the first step, he proposed, toward fully implementing the 1993 UN resolution calling for a Fissile Material Cutoff Treaty (FISSBAN). Unless some such proposal is implemented, the prospects for long-term human survival are not bright.

To date, ElBaradei's proposal has been accepted by only one state, to my knowledge: Iran, in February (2006) in an interview with Ali Larijani, Iran's chief nuclear negotiator.[4]

Again, there is only one way to discover whether the Iranian stand is intended seriously: pursue it. At least, report it so that it will be possible to pressure Washington to determine whether it is serious.

The Bush administration rejects a verifiable FISSBAN—and stands nearly alone, a familiar posture. In November 2004 the UN Committee on Disarmament voted in favor of a verifiable FISSBAN. The vote was 147 to 1 (United States), with two abstentions: Israel and Britain. In the debate, the British Ambassador stated that Britain supports the treaty, but could not vote for it because this version "divided the international community": 147 to 1. The Blair government's priorities shine forth bright and clear.

Last year (2005) there was a vote on the treaty in the full UN General Assembly. The vote was 179 to 2, Israel and Britain again abstaining. The United States was joined by Palau.

There are ways to mitigate and probably end these crises. The first is to call off the very credible U.S. and Israeli threats that virtually urge Iran to develop nuclear weapons as a deterrent (and are, if anyone cares, a serious violation of the UN Charter).

A second step would be to join the rest of the world in accepting a verifiable FISSBAN treaty, as well as ElBaradei's proposal, or something similar.

A third step would be to live up to Article VI of the Nuclear Non-Proliferation Treaty, which obligates the nuclear states to take "good faith" efforts to eliminate nuclear weapons, a binding legal obligation, as the World Court determined. None of the nuclear states has lived up to that obligation, but the United States is far in the lead in violating it.

Even steps in these directions would mitigate the upcoming crisis with Iran. Above all, it is important to heed the words of Mohamed ElBaradei: "There is no military solution to this situation. It is inconceivable. The only durable solution is a negotiated solution." And it is within reach.[5]

NOTES

1. See William A. Dorman and Mansour Farhang, *The U.S. Press and Iran* (1987). For review and more general context, see *Necessary Illusions*, Appendix V.3.
2. For more recent details, see Glenn Kessler, "2003 Memo Says Iranian Leaders Backed Talks," *Washington Post*, February 14, 2007. The text of the Iranian proposal appears on the *Washington Post*'s Web site, confirming the reports.
3. See Selig Harrison, "It is time to put security issues on the table with Iran," *Financial Times*, January 18, 2006.
4. See Larijani, interview on French radio, February 16, 2006. Press release, Government of Iran, February 17, 2006. See also Gareth Smyth et al., "Iran raises hopes of nuclear settlement," *Financial Times*, February 12, 2007.
5. The first major poll on these matters (PIPA, February 2007) reveals that if the U.S. and Iran were functioning demo-

cratic societies, in which public opinion influences policy, the outstanding issues could probably be readily resolved. Iranians and Americans are largely in agreement "on nearly all the major questions related to nuclear weapons proliferation," the study reveals: specifically, on Iran's right to nuclear power but not nuclear weapons, elimination of all nuclear weapons, and a "nuclear-weapons-free zone in the Middle East that would include both Islamic countries and Israel." Washington flatly rejects these positions, with strong bipartisan support. That is yet another illustration of the vast gap between public opinion and public policy. On this matter, see *Failed States* and Benjamin Page (with Marshall Bouton), *The Foreign Policy Disconnect* (2006). The "disconnect" extends to the most crucial questions of domestic policy.

Viewing Lebanon as if through a Bombsight

AUGUST 24, 2006

In Lebanon, a fragile truce remains in effect—yet another in a decades-long series of cease-fires between Israel and its adversaries in a cycle that regularly returns to warfare, carnage and human misery.

Let's describe the current crisis for what it is: a U.S.-Israeli invasion of Lebanon, with only a cynical pretense to legitimacy. In the background, as in the past, lies the Israeli-Palestinian conflict.

This is not the first time that Israel has invaded Lebanon to eliminate an alleged threat. In no case was there a credible pretext. That was clearly true of the most important of the U.S.-backed Israeli invasions of Lebanon, in 1982. Reporting and commentary in the U.S. commonly describe the invasion as a response to Palestinian terror, rocketing of the Galilee, and so on. That is sheer fabrication. The Palestine Liberation Organization (PLO) was adhering rigorously to a U.S.-initiated cease-fire, despite repeated and often murderous Israeli attacks in Lebanon in an attempt to elicit some act that could serve as a pretext for the planned invasion. There were only two light reactions, recognized to be mere warnings. Israel then invaded on a concocted pretext in June 1982, with the backing of the Reagan administration. Within Israel, at the highest military and political echelons, the invasion, which killed some 15-

20,000 people and left much of the country in ruins, was described as a war for the West Bank. It was undertaken to end the Palestine Liberation Organization's annoying calls for a diplomatic settlement.

Despite many different circumstances, the July (2006) invasion falls into a similar pattern. In this case, the pretext was the capture of two Israeli soldiers in a cross-border Hezbollah attack. The harshest Western criticism of the devastating U.S.-Israeli invasion was that it was "disproportionate." But the reaction is pure cynicism. For decades, Israel had been kidnapping and killing civilians in Lebanon or on the high seas, Lebanese and Palestinian, holding them in Israel for long periods, sometimes as hostages, sometimes in secret torture chambers like Camp 1391.[1]

There has been no call for invasion of Israel. Or of the U.S., which provides the necessary support for such actions.

The same is true of the sharp escalation of the attack against Gaza after the capture of Corporal Gilad Shalit on June 25, 2006. The U.S. and its allies professed deep shock at this terrible crime and, with the usual reservations about how it might be disproportionate, lent their support to the savage Israeli reaction—for example, the destruction of the power plant to deprive the population of electricity, water, sewage disposal; the regular sonic booms at night to terrorize children; the sharp increase in killing civilians; and much more that renders the state "no longer distinguishable from a terror organization" as it turns its helpless victim into "a withered, blighted garden, enveloped in grief and suffering."[2]

The fraudulence of the reaction was even more transparent than usual in this case. One day before, on June 24, 2006, Israel had kidnapped two civilians in Gaza, the Muammar brothers, a far more serious crime than capturing a soldier, and abducted them to Israel in violation of the Geneva Conventions. They disappeared into the Israeli prison system, where close to 1,000 people are held without charge, hence kidnapped. There was no reaction in the West to Israel's June 24 kidnapping, in fact barely even any notice.

What would break the cycle? The basic outlines of a solution to the Israel-Palestine conflict are familiar and have been supported by a broad international consensus for thirty years: a two-state settlement on the international border, perhaps with minor and mutual adjustments.

The Arab states formally accepted this proposal in 2002, as the Palestinians had, long before. Hezbollah leader Sayyed Hassan Nasrallah has made it clear that though this solution is not Hezbollah's preference, they will not disrupt it. Iran's "supreme leader" Ayatollah Khamenei recently reaffirmed that Iran, too, supports this settlement. Hamas has indicated clearly that it is prepared to negotiate for a settlement in these terms as well.

The United States and Israel continue to block this political settlement, as they have done for thirty years, with brief and inconsequential exceptions. Denial may be preferred at home, but the victims do not enjoy that luxury.

U.S.-Israeli rejectionism is not only in words, but more important, in actions. With decisive U.S. backing, Israel has been systematically pursuing its program of annexation, dismemberment of shrinking Palestinian territories, and imprisonment of what remains by taking over the Jordan Valley—the "convergence" program that is, astonishingly, called "courageous withdrawal" in the United States.

In consequence, the Palestinians are facing national destruction. The most meaningful support for Palestinians is from Hezbollah, which was formed in reaction to the 1982 invasion. Hezbollah won considerable prestige by leading the effort to force Israel to withdraw from Lebanon in 2000. Also, like other Islamic movements, including Hamas, Hezbollah has gained popular support by providing social services to the poor.

To U.S. and Israeli planners it therefore follows that Hezbollah must be severely weakened or destroyed—just as the PLO had to be evicted from Lebanon in 1982. But Hezbollah is so deeply embedded within Lebanese society that it cannot be eradicated without destroying much of Lebanon as well—hence the scale of the attack on the country's population and infrastructure.

In keeping with a familiar pattern, the aggression is sharply increasing the support for Hezbollah, not only in the Arab and Muslim worlds beyond but also in Lebanon itself.

Late last month (July 2006), polls revealed that 87 percent of Lebanese support Hezbollah's resistance against the invasion, including 80 percent of Christians and Druze. Even Cardinal Mar Nasrallah Boutros Sfeir, the Maronite Catholic patriarch, the spiritual leader of the most pro-Western sector in Lebanon, joined Sunni and Shiite religious leaders in a statement condemning the "aggression" and hailing "the resistance, mainly led by Hezbollah." The poll also found that 90 percent of Lebanese regard the United States as "complicit in Israel's war crimes against the Lebanese people."

Amal Saad-Ghorayeb, Lebanon's leading academic scholar on Hezbollah, observes that "these findings are all the more significant when compared to the results of a similar survey conducted just five months ago, which showed that only 58 percent of all Lebanese believed Hezbollah had the right to remain armed, and hence, continue its resistance activity."

The dynamics are familiar. Rami G. Khouri, an editor of Lebanon's *Daily Star*, writes that "the Lebanese and Palestinians have responded to Israel's persistent and increasingly savage attacks against entire civilian populations by creating parallel or alternative leaderships that can protect them and deliver essential services."

Such popular forces will only gain in power and become more extremist if the United States and Israel persist in demolishing any hope of Palestinian national rights and in destroying Lebanon.

In the current crisis even King Abdullah of Saudi Arabia, Washington's oldest (and most important) ally in the region, was compelled to say, "If the peace option is rejected due to the Israeli arrogance, then only the war option remains, and no one knows the repercussions befalling the region, including wars and conflict that will spare no one, including those whose military power is now tempting them to play with fire."

It is no secret that Israel has helped to destroy secular Arab nationalism and to create Hezbollah and Hamas, just as U.S. violence has expedited the rise of extremist Islamic fundamentalism and jihadi terror. The latest adventure is likely to create new generations of bitter and angry jihadis, just as the invasion of Iraq did.

Israeli writer Uri Avnery observed that Israeli Chief of Staff Dan Halutz, former air force commander, "views the world below through a bombsight." Much the same is true of Rumsfeld-Cheney-Rice and other top Bush administration planners. As history reveals, that view of the world is not uncommon among those who wield most of the means of violence.

Saad-Ghorayeb describes the current violence in "apocalyptic terms," warning that possibly "all hell would be let loose" if the outcome of the U.S.-Israel campaign leaves a situation in which "the Shiite community is seething with resentment at Israel, the United States and the government that it perceives as its betrayer."

The core issue—the Israel-Palestine conflict—can be dealt with by diplomacy, if the United States and Israel abandon their rejectionist commitments. Other outstanding problems in the region are also susceptible to negotiation and diplomacy. Their success can never be guaranteed. But we can be reasonably confident that viewing the world through a bombsight will bring further misery and suffering, perhaps even in "apocalyptic terms."

NOTES

1. On the prisons, see Aviv Lavie, "Inside Israel's secret prison," *Haaretz*, August 22, 2003; Jonathan Cook, "Facility 1391: Israel's Guantanamo," *Le Monde diplomatique*, November 2003; and Chris McGreal, "Facility 1391: Israel's secret prison," *Guardian* (UK), November 14, 2003.
2. Gideon Levy, *Haaretz*, July 2, August 18, 2006. B'Tselem, *Act of Vengeance: Israel's Bombing of the Gaza Power Plant and its Effects* (September 2006). This is, of course, only the barest sample.

Latin America Declares its Independence

SEPTEMBER 6, 2006

Five centuries after the European conquests, South America is reasserting its independence. From Venezuela to Argentina, much of the region is rising to overthrow the legacy of external domination of the past centuries and the cruel and destructive social forms that they have helped to establish.

The mechanisms of imperial control—violence and economic warfare, hardly a distant memory in Latin America—are losing their effectiveness, a sign of the shift toward independence. Washington is now compelled to tolerate governments that in the past would have drawn intervention or reprisal.

Throughout the region a vibrant array of popular movements provides the basis for a meaningful democracy. The indigenous populations, as if in a rediscovery of their pre-Columbian legacy, are becoming active and influential, particularly in Bolivia and Ecuador.

These developments are in part the result of a phenomenon that has been observed for some years by specialists and polling organizations in Latin America: As the elected governments became more formally democratic, citizens have expressed an increasing disillusionment with the way democracy functions and "lack of faith" in the democratic institutions. They have sought to construct democratic systems based on popular participation rather than elite and foreign domination.

A persuasive explanation for the decline of faith in existing democratic institutions has been offered by Argentine political scientist Atilio Borón, who observed that the new wave of democratization in Latin America coincided with externally mandated economic "reforms" that undermine effective democracy: the neoliberal "Washington consensus," virtually every element of which undermines democracy, and which has also led to economic disaster in Latin America, as in other regions that rigorously followed the rules.

The concepts of democracy and development are closely related in many respects. One is that they have a common enemy: loss of sovereignty. In a world of nation-states, it is true by definition that decline of sovereignty entails decline of democracy, and decline in ability to conduct social and economic policy. That in turn harms development, a conclusion confirmed by centuries of economic history.

The same historical record reveals that loss of sovereignty consistently leads to imposed liberalization, of course in the interests of those with the power to impose this social and economic regime. In recent years, the imposed regime is commonly called "neoliberalism." It is not a very good term: The socioeconomic regime is not new, and it is not liberal, at least as the concept was understood by classical liberals.

In the United States, faith in institutions has also been declining steadily, and for good reasons. A huge gulf has opened between public opinion and public policy, rarely reported, though people cannot fail to be aware that their policy choices are disregarded.

It is instructive to compare the recent presidential elections in the richest country of the world and the poorest country in South America—Bolivia.

As noted earlier, in November 2004 U.S. voters had a choice

between two candidates from the upper reaches of privileged elites. Their programs were similar, consistent with the needs of their primary constituency: wealth and privilege. Studies of public opinion revealed that on a host of major issues, both parties are well to the right of the general population, the Bush administration dramatically so. In part for these reasons, issues are removed from the electoral agenda. Few voters even knew the stand of the candidates on issues. Candidates are packaged and sold like toothpaste and cars and lifestyle drugs, and by the same industries, dedicated to delusion and deceit.

For contrast, consider Bolivia and Evo Morales's election last December (2005). Voters were familiar with the issues, very real and important ones like domestic control over natural gas and other resources, which has overwhelming popular support. Indigenous rights, women's rights, land rights, and water rights are on the political agenda, among many other critical issues that had been the focus of constant struggle by popular organizations. The population chose someone from their own ranks, not a representative of narrow sectors of privilege. There was real participation, not just pushing a lever once every few years.

The comparison, and it is not the only one, raises some questions about where programs of "democracy promotion" are needed.

In the context of these developments, Latin America may come to terms with some of its severe internal problems. The region is notorious for the rapacity of its wealthy classes and their freedom from social responsibility.

Comparative studies of Latin American and East Asian economic development are revealing in this respect. Latin America has close to the world's worst record for inequality, East Asia the best. The same holds for education, health, and social welfare generally. Imports to Latin America have been heavily skewed toward consumption by the rich; in East Asia, toward productive investment. Capital flight from Latin America has approached the scale of the debt—suggesting a way to overcome this crushing burden. In East Asia, capital flight has been tightly controlled.

Latin American economies have also been more open to foreign investment than Asia. Since the 1950s, foreign multinationals have controlled far larger shares of industrial production in Latin America than in the East Asian success stories, according to the UN Conference on Trade and Development (UNCTAD). The World Bank reported that foreign investment and privatization have tended to substitute for other capital flows in Latin America, transferring control and sending profits abroad, unlike East Asia.

Meanwhile new socioeconomic programs under way in Latin America are reversing patterns that trace back to the Spanish conquests—with Latin American elites and economies linked to the imperial powers but not to one another.

Of course this shift is highly unwelcome in Washington, for the traditional reasons: The United States has expected to rely on Latin America as a secure base for resources, markets, and investment opportunities. And as planners have long emphasized, if this hemisphere is out of control, how can the United States hope to resist defiance elsewhere?

Alternatives for the Americas

DECEMBER 29, 2006

This month a coincidence of birth and death signaled a transition for South America and indeed for the world.

Former Chilean dictator Augusto Pinochet died even as leaders of South American nations concluded a two-day summit meeting in Cochabamba, Bolivia, hosted by Bolivian president Evo Morales, where the participants and the agenda represented the antithesis of Pinochet and his era of neo-Nazi National Security States—supported and sometimes installed by the master of the hemisphere—a plague of terror, torture, and general savagery that spread from Argentina through Central America.

In the Cochabamba Declaration, the presidents and envoys of twelve nations agreed to study the idea of forming a continentwide community similar to the European Union.

The Declaration marks another stage in recent moves toward regional integration in South America, 500 years after the European conquests. The subcontinent, from Venezuela to Argentina, may yet present an example to the world on how to create an alternative future from a legacy of empire and terror.

The United States has long dominated the region by two major methods: violence and economic strangulation. Quite generally, international affairs have more than a slight resemblance to the Mafia. The Godfather does not take it lightly when he is crossed, even by a small storekeeper—as Latin Americans know all too well.

Previous attempts at independence have been crushed, partly because of a lack of regional cooperation. Without it, threats can be handled one by one.

To the United States, the real enemy has always been independent nationalism, particularly when it threatens to become a "contagious example," to borrow Henry Kissinger's characterization of democratic socialism in Chile—cured of the infection on 9/11 1973, in the manner described earlier.

Among the leaders at Cochabamba was Chilean president Michelle Bachelet. Like Allende, she is a socialist and a physician. She also is a former exile and political prisoner. Her father was a general who died in prison after being tortured.

At Cochabamba, Morales and Venezuelan president Hugo Chávez celebrated a new joint venture, a gas separation project in Bolivia. Such cooperation strengthens the region's role as a major player in global energy. Venezuela is already the only Latin American member of OPEC, with by far the largest proven oil reserves outside the Middle East. Chávez envisions Petroamerica, an integrated energy system of the kind that China is trying to initiate in Asia.

The new Ecuadorian president Rafael Correa proposed a land-and-river trade link from the Brazilian Amazon rain forest to Ecuador's Pacific Coast—a South American counterpart to the Panama Canal. Other promising developments include Telesur, an effort to break the Western media monopoly. Brazilian president Lula da Silva called on fellow leaders to overcome historical differences and unite the continent, however difficult the task.

Integration is a prerequisite for genuine independence. The colonial history—Spain, England, other European powers, the United States—not only divided countries from one another but also left a sharp internal division within the countries, between a wealthy small elite and a mass of impoverished people.

The correlation to race is fairly close. Typically, the rich elite was white, European, westernized, and the poor were indigenous, Indian, black and intermingled. The mostly white elites had few interrelations with the other countries of the region. They were oriented to the West, not to their own societies in the South.

Because of the new developments in South America, the United States has been forced to adjust policy. The governments that now have U.S. support—like Brazil, under Lula—might well have been overthrown in the past, as was Brazilian president João Goulart in a U.S.-backed coup in 1964.

The main economic controls in recent years have come from the International Monetary Fund, which is virtually a branch of the U.S. Treasury Department. Argentina was the poster child of the IMF—until the crash of 2001. Argentina recovered, but by violating IMF rules, refusing to pay its debts and buying up what remained of the debt—partly with the help of Venezuela, in another form of cooperation.

Brazil, in its own way, has moved in the same direction to free itself from the IMF. Bolivia had been an obedient student of the IMF for about twenty-five years and ended up with per capita income lower than when it started. Now Bolivia is getting rid of the IMF, too, again with Venezuelan support.

In South America, the United States has been forced to reconcile itself to center-left governments, and has shifted to a distinction between the good guys and the bad guys. Brazil's Lula is one of the good guys. Chávez and Morales are the bad guys.

To maintain Washington's party line, though, it's necessary to finesse some of the facts. For example, the fact that when

Lula was re-elected in October (2006), one of his first acts was to fly to Caracas to support Chávez's electoral campaign. Also, Lula dedicated a Brazilian project in Venezuela, a bridge over the Orinoco River, and discussed other joint projects.

This month (December 2006), MERCOSUR, the South American trading bloc, continued the dialogue on South American unity at its semiannual meeting in Brazil, where Lula inaugurated the MERCOSUR Parliament—another hopeful sign of deliverance from the demons of the past.

The barriers to the dual integration—among countries, and within them—are daunting, but the steps that are being taken have promise, not least because of the role of dynamic mass popular movements, laying the basis for authentic democracy and desperately needed social change.

What is at Stake in Iraq

JANUARY 30, 2007

In the West, some of the most important information about Iraq remains either ignored or unspoken. Unless it is taken into account, proposals about U.S. policies in Iraq will be neither morally nor strategically sound.

For example, one of the least noticed recent news stories from the tortured land of Iraq was among the most illuminating: a poll in Baghdad, Anbar, and Najaf on the invasion and its consequences. "About 90 percent of Iraqis feel the situation in the country was better before the U.S.-led invasion than it is today," United Press International reported on the survey, which was conducted in November 2006 by the Baghdad-based Iraq Center for Research and Strategic Studies. "Nearly half of the respondents favored an immediate withdrawal of U.S.-led troops," reported the *Daily Star* in Beirut, Lebanon. Another 20 percent favored a phased withdrawal starting right away. (A U.S. State Department poll, also ignored, found that two-thirds of Baghdadis want immediate withdrawal.)

Generally, however, public opinion—in Iraq, the United States or elsewhere—is not considered relevant to policy-makers, unless it may impede their preferred choices. These are just further indications of the deep contempt for democracy on the part of planners and their acolytes, standard accompaniments of a flood of lofty rhetoric about love of democracy and messianic missions to promote it.

U.S. polls show majority opposition to the war, but they receive limited attention and scarcely enter into policy planning, or even critique of planning. The most prominent recent critique was the report of the Baker-Hamilton Iraq Study Group, widely acclaimed as a valuable critical corrective to the policies of the George W. Bush administration, which immediately dismissed the report to oblivion. One notable feature of the report is its lack of concern for the will of the Iraqi people. The report cites some of the polls of Iraqi sentiment, but only in regard to the safety of U.S. forces. The report's implicit assumption is that policy should be designed for U.S. government interests, not those of Iraqis; or of Americans, also ignored.

The report makes no inquiry into those guiding interests, or why the United States invaded, or why it fears a sovereign and more or less democratic Iraq, though the answers are not hard to find. The real reason for the invasion, surely, is that Iraq has the second largest oil reserves in the world, very cheap to exploit, and is at the heart of the world's major hydrocarbon resources. The issue is not access to those resources but control of them (and for the energy corporations, profit). As Vice President Dick Cheney observed last May (2006), control over energy resources provides "tools of intimidation or blackmail"—in the hands of others, that is.

Buried in the study is the expected recommendation to allow corporate (meaning mostly U.S.-U.K.) control over Iraq's energy resources. In the more delicate phrasing of the study, "The United States should assist Iraqi leaders to reorganize the national oil industry as a commercial enterprise, in order to enhance efficiency, transparency, and accountability."

Because of its systematic unwillingness to discuss such crass matters, the Study Group is unable to face the reality of U.S.

policy choices in the face of the catastrophe that the invasion has created, already discussed.

The Baker-Hamilton report's central focus is withdrawal of U.S. forces from Iraq: more specifically, their withdrawal from direct combat, though the proposals were hedged with many qualifications and evasions. The report has a few words urging the president to announce that the United States does not intend a permanent military presence in Iraq, but without a call to terminate construction of military bases, so such a declaration is not likely to be taken seriously by Iraqis.

The report appears to assume (by omission) that logistics, the backbone of a modern army, should remain under U.S. control, and that combat units must remain for "force protection"—including protection of U.S. combat forces embedded in Iraqi units—in a country where 60 percent of the population, and many more in Arab Iraq where forces are actually deployed, regard them as a legitimate target, the soldiers in their units for example.

There is also no discussion of the fact that the U.S. will, of course, retain total control of airspace and therefore might be tempted to resort to the tactics it used in the later stages of the Indochina wars as troops were being withdrawn, an ominous prospect discussed in a very important article by two leading Cambodia specialists, Taylor Owen and Ben Kiernan (director of the Yale University Genocide project), "Bombs over Cambodia," *Walrus* (Canada), October 2006. It was well known that reduction of ground forces from South Vietnam was accompanied by acceleration of the merciless bombing, particularly of northern Laos and Cambodia. But they provide startling new information about its scale and consequences. The new data reveal that the bombing of Cambodia was five times as great as the incredible level that had been reported earlier, meaning that the bombing of rural Cambodia exceeded the total bombing by allied forces throughout World War II. The new material substantially reinforces earlier estimates of the impact of the bombing. In the authors' words, "Civilian casualties in Cambodia drove an enraged populace into the arms of an insurgency that had enjoyed relatively little support until the bombing began, setting in motion . . . the rapid rise of the Khmer Rouge, and ultimately the Cambodian genocide." Nixon's orders for the bombing attack were transmitted by Henry Kissinger, with the words "Anything that flies, on anything that moves"—one of the most explicit calls for genocide in the archives of any state. Kissinger's orders had been mentioned in the *New York Times* (Elizabeth Becker, "Kissinger Tapes Describe Crises, War and Stark Photos of Abuse," May 27, 2004), eliciting no detectable reaction. Silence also greeted the horrendous new revelations. The null reactions provide additional evidence of the actual concern for Cambodians on the part of those in the West who were gleefully exploiting their plight for personal gain and in the service of power while the Khmer Rouge atrocities were underway, with no suggestion as to what to do about them—in sharp contrast to their reaction to comparable massacres for which we had primary responsibility and could therefore terminate, if we chose.[1]

One can hardly dismiss lightly the Owen-Kiernan concerns about what might unfold in Iraq, in the light of such recent precedents as these.

Some observers fear that a U.S. pullout from Iraq would lead to a full-fledged civil war and the country's deterioration. As for the consequences of a withdrawal, we are entitled to our personal judgments, all of them as uninformed and dubious as those of U.S. intelligence. But these judgments do not matter.

What matters is what Iraqis think. Or rather, that is what should matter.

If the consistent results of many polls are considered insufficient, the question of withdrawal could even be submitted to a referendum, conducted under international supervision to minimize coercion by the occupying forces and their Iraqi clients.

Now, contrary to the Baker-Hamilton report (and to Iraqi and U.S. public opinion), the Washington plan is to "surge"— to introduce more troops into Iraq. Few military analysts or Middle East specialists expect such tactics to succeed, but that is plainly not the primary issue, unless we agree that the only question that can be raised is whether U.S. aggression can succeed in its goals. No one should underestimate the force of the long-standing goal of U.S. foreign policy to sustain its control over this region's crucial resources. Authentic Iraqi sovereignty will not easily be tolerated by the occupying power, nor can it or neighboring states tolerate Iraq's deterioration, or a potential regional war in the aftermath.

NOTES

1. For a review of this sordid episode of intellectual history, and many others like it, see Edward Herman and Noam Chomsky, *Manufacturing Consent* (1988, updated 2002) and sources cited, particularly our *Political Economy of Human Rights*, two volumes (1979).

The Cold War Between Washington and Tehran

MARCH 5, 2007

In the energy-rich Middle East, only two countries have failed to subordinate themselves to Washington's basic demands: Iran and Syria. Accordingly both are enemies, Iran by far the more important.

As was the norm during the Cold War, resort to violence is regularly justified as a reaction to the malign influence of the main enemy, often on the flimsiest of pretexts. Unsurprisingly, as Bush sends more troops to Iraq, tales surface of Iranian interference in the internal affairs of Iraq—a country otherwise free from any foreign interference, on the tacit assumption that Washington rules the world.

In the Cold War-like mentality that prevails in Washington, Tehran is portrayed as the pinnacle in the so-called Shiite Crescent that stretches from Iran to Hezbollah in Lebanon, through Shiite southern Iraq and Syria. And again unsurprisingly, the "surge" in Iraq and escalation of threats and accusations against Iran is accompanied by grudging willingness to attend a conference of regional powers, with the agenda limited to Iraq—more narrowly, to attaining U.S. goals in Iraq.

Presumably this minimal gesture toward diplomacy is intended to allay the growing fears and anger elicited by Washington's heightened aggressiveness, with forces deployed in position to attack Iran and regular provocations and threats.

For the United States, the primary issue in the Middle East has been and remains effective control of its unparalleled energy resources. Access is a secondary matter. Once the oil is on the seas it goes anywhere. Control is understood to be an instrument of global dominance.

Iranian influence in the "crescent" challenges U.S. control. By an accident of geography, the world's major oil resources are in largely Shiite areas of the Middle East: southern Iraq, adjacent regions of Saudi Arabia and Iran, with some of the major reserves of natural gas as well. Washington's worst nightmare would be a loose Shiite alliance controlling most of the world's oil and independent of the United States.

Such a bloc, if it emerges, might even join the Asian Energy Security Grid and Shanghai Cooperation Organization (SCO), based in China. Iran, which already had observer status, is to be admitted as a member of the SCO. The Hong Kong *South China Morning Post* reported in June 2006 that "Iranian President Mahmoud Ahmadinejad stole the limelight at the annual meeting of the Shanghai Co-operation Organisation (SCO) by calling on the group to unite against other countries as his nation faces criticism over its nuclear programme." The non-aligned movement meanwhile affirmed Iran's "inalienable right" to pursue these programs, and the SCO (which includes the states of Central Asia) "called on the United States to set a deadline for the withdrawal of military installations from all member states."[1]

If the Bush planners bring that about, they will have seriously undermined the U.S. position of power in the world.

To Washington, Tehran's principal offense has been its defiance, going back to the overthrow of the Shah in 1979 and the hostage crisis at the U.S. embassy. The grim U.S. role in Iran in earlier years is excised from history. In retribution for Iranian defiance, Washington quickly turned to support for Saddam Hussein's aggression against Iran, which left hundreds of thousands dead and the country in ruins. Then came murderous sanctions, and under Bush, rejection of Iranian diplomatic efforts in favor of increasing threats of direct attack.

Last July (2006), Israel invaded Lebanon, the fifth invasion since 1978. As before, U.S. support for the aggression was a critical factor, the pretexts quickly collapse on inspection, and the consequences for the people of Lebanon are severe. Among the reasons for the U.S.-Israel invasion is that Hezbollah's rockets could be a deterrent to a potential U.S.-Israeli attack on Iran.

Despite the saber-rattling, it is, I suspect, unlikely that the Bush administration will attack Iran. The world is strongly opposed. Seventy-five percent of Americans favor diplomacy over military threats against Iran, and as noted earlier, Americans and Iranians largely agree on nuclear issues. Polls by Terror Free Tomorrow reveal that "Despite a deep historical enmity between Iran's Persian Shiite population and the predominantly Sunni population of its ethnically diverse Arab, Turkish and Pakistani neighbors, the largest percentage of people in these countries favor accepting a nuclear-armed Iran over any American military action." It appears that the U.S. military and intelligence community is also opposed to an attack.

Iran cannot defend itself against U.S. attack, but it can respond in other ways, among them by inciting even more havoc in Iraq. Some issue warnings that are far more grave, among them by the respected British military historian Corelli Barnett, who writes that "an attack on Iran would effectively launch World War III."

The Bush administration has left disasters almost everywhere it has turned, from post-Katrina New Orleans to Iraq. In desperation to salvage something, the administration might undertake the risk of even greater disasters.

Meanwhile Washington may be seeking to destabilize Iran from within.[2] The ethnic mix in Iran is complex; much of the population isn't Persian. There are secessionist tendencies and it is likely that Washington is trying to stir them up—in Khuzestan on the Gulf, for example, where Iran's oil is concentrated, a region that is largely Arab, not Persian.

Threat escalation also serves to pressure others to join U.S. efforts to strangle Iran economically, with predictable success in Europe. Another predictable consequence, presumably intended, is to induce the Iranian leadership to be as harsh and repressive as possible, fomenting disorder and perhaps resistance while undermining efforts of courageous Iranian reformers, who are bitterly protesting Washington's tactics. It is also necessary to demonize the leadership. In the West, any wild statement of Iran's president, Mahmoud Ahmadinejad, immediately gets circulated in headlines, dubiously translated. But as is well known, Ahmadinejad has no control over foreign policy, which is in the hands of his superior, the Supreme Leader Ayatollah Ali Khamenei.

The U.S. media tend to ignore Khamenei's statements, especially if they are conciliatory. For example, it's widely reported when Ahmadinejad says that Israel shouldn't exist—but there is silence when Khamenei says that Iran "shares a common view with Arab countries on the most important Islamic-Arabic issue, namely the issue of Palestine," which would appear to mean that Iran accepts the Arab League position: full normalization of relations with Israel in terms of the international consensus on a two-state settlement that the U.S. and Israel continue to resist, almost alone.[3]

The U.S. invasion of Iraq virtually instructed Iran to develop a nuclear deterrent. Israeli military historian Martin van Creveld writes that after the U.S. invasion of Iraq, "had the Iranians not tried to build nuclear weapons, they would be crazy." The message of the invasion, loud and clear, was that the U.S. will attack at will, as long as the target is defenseless. Now Iran is ringed by U.S. military forces in Afghanistan, Iraq, Turkey and the Persian Gulf and close by are nuclear-armed Pakistan and particularly Israel, the regional superpower, thanks to U.S. support.

As already discussed, Iranian efforts to negotiate outstanding issues were rebuffed by Washington, and an EU-Iranian agreement was apparently undermined by Washington's refusal to withdraw threats of attack. A genuine interest in preventing the development of nuclear weapons in Iran—and the escalating warlike tension in the region—would lead Washington to implement the EU bargain, agree to meaningful negotiations and join with others to move toward integrating Iran into the international economic system, in accord with public opinion in the United States, Iran, neighboring states, and virtually the entire rest of the world.

NOTES

1. See M. K. Bhadrakumar, "China, Russia welcome Iran into the fold," *Asia Times*, April 18, 2006. Bill Savadove, "President of Iran calls for unity against west," *South China Morning Post*, June 16, 2006; "Non-aligned nations back Iran's nuclear program," *Japan Economic Newswire*, May 30, 2006; Edward Cody, "Iran Seeks Aid in Asia In Resisting the West," *Washington Post*, June 15, 2006.

2. See, among others, William Lowther and Colin Freeman, "US funds terror groups to sow chaos in Iran," *Sunday Telegraph*, February 25, 2007.

3. For Khamenei's statement, see "Leader Attends Memorial Ceremony Marking the 17th Departure Anniversary of Imam Khomeini," June 4, 2006. http://www.khamenei.ir/EN/News/detail.jsp?id=20060604A.

The Great Soul of Power

JULY 13, 2006

It is a challenging task to select a few themes from the remarkable range of the work and life of Edward Said. I will keep to two: the culture of empire, and the responsibility of intellectuals or those whom we call "intellectuals" if they have the privilege and resources to enter the public arena.

The phrase "responsibility of intellectuals" conceals a crucial ambiguity: It blurs the distinction between "ought" and "is." In terms of "ought," their responsibility should be exactly the same as that of any decent human being, though greater: Privilege confers opportunity, and opportunity confers moral responsibility.

We rightly condemn the obedient intellectuals of brutal and violent states for their "conformist subservience to those in power." I am borrowing the phrase from Hans Morgenthau, a founder of international relations theory.

Morgenthau was referring, however, not to the commissar class of the totalitarian enemy, but to Western intellectuals, whose crime is far greater, because they cannot plead fear but only cowardice and subordination to power. He was describing what "is," not what "ought" to be.

The history of intellectuals is written by intellectuals, so not surprisingly, they are portrayed as defenders of right and justice, upholding the highest values and confronting power and evil with admirable courage and integrity. The record reveals a rather different picture.

The pattern of "conformist subservience" goes back to the earliest recorded history. It was the man who "corrupted the youth of Athens" with "false gods" who drank the hemlock, not those who worshipped the true gods of the doctrinal system. A large part of the Bible is devoted to people who condemned the crimes of state and immoral practices. They are called "prophets," a dubious translation of an obscure word. In contemporary terms, they were "dissident intellectuals." There is no need to review how they were treated: miserably, the norm for dissidents.

There were also intellectuals who were greatly respected in the era of the prophets: the flatterers at the court. The Gospels warn of "false prophets, who come to you in sheep's clothing, but inwardly are ravening wolves. By their fruits ye shall know them."

The dogmas that uphold the nobility of state power are nearly unassailable, despite the occasional errors and failures that critics allow themselves to condemn. A prevailing truth was expressed by U.S. President John Adams two centuries ago: "Power always thinks it has a great soul and vast views beyond the comprehension of the weak." That is the deep root of the combination of savagery and self-righteousness that infects the imperial mentality—and in some measure, every structure of authority and domination.

We can add that reverence for that great soul is the normal stance of intellectual elites, who regularly add that they should hold the levers of control, or at least be close by.

One common expression of this prevailing view is that there are two categories of intellectuals: the "technocratic and policy-oriented intellectuals"—responsible, sober, constructive—and the "value-oriented intellectuals," a sinister grouping who pose a threat to democracy as they "devote themselves to the derogation of leadership, the challenging of authority, and the unmasking of established institutions."

I am quoting from a 1975 study by the Trilateral Commission—liberal internationalists from the United States, Europe, and Japan. They were reflecting on the "crisis of democracy" that developed in the 1960s, when normally passive and apathetic sectors of the population, called "the special interests," sought to enter the political arena to advance their concerns.

Those improper initiatives created what the study called a "crisis of democracy," in which the proper functioning of the state was threatened by "excessive democracy." To overcome this crisis, the special interests must be restored to their proper function as passive observers, so that the "technocratic and policy-oriented intellectuals" can do their constructive work.

The disruptive special interests are women, the young, the elderly, workers, farmers, minorities, majorities—in short, the population. Only one special interest is not mentioned in the study: the corporate sector. But that makes sense. The corporate sector represents the "national interest," and naturally there can be no question that state power protects the national interest.

The reactions to this dangerous civilizing and democratizing trend have set their stamp on the contemporary era.

For those who want to understand what is likely to lie ahead, it is of prime importance to look closely at the long-standing principles that animate the decisions and actions of the powerful—in today's world, primarily the United States.

Though only one of three major power centers in economic and most other dimensions, it surpasses any power in history in its military dominance, which is rapidly expanding, and it can generally rely on the support of Europe and Japan, the second-largest industrial economy.

There is a clear doctrine on the general contours of U.S. foreign policy. It reigns in Western journalism and almost all scholarship, even among critics of policies. The major theme is "American exceptionalism": the thesis that the United States is unlike other great powers, past and present, because it has a "transcendent purpose": "the establishment of equality in freedom in America," and indeed throughout the world, since "the arena within which the United States must defend and promote its purpose has become worldwide."

The version of the thesis I have just quoted is particularly interesting because of its source: Hans Morgenthau. But this quote is from the Kennedy years, before the Vietnam War erupted in full savagery. The previous quote was from 1970, when he had shifted to a more critical phase in his thinking.

Figures of the highest intelligence and moral integrity have championed the stance of "exceptionalism." Consider John Stuart Mill's classic essay, "A Few Words on Non-Intervention."

Mill raised the question whether England should intervene in the ugly world or keep to its own business and let the barbarians carry out their savagery. His conclusion, nuanced and complex, was that England should intervene, even though by doing so, it will endure the "obloquy" and abuse of Europeans, who will "seek base motives" because they cannot comprehend that England is "a novelty in the world," an angelic power that seeks nothing for itself and acts only for the benefit of others. Though England selflessly bears the cost of intervention, it shares the benefits of its labors with others equally.

Exceptionalism seems to be close to universal. I suspect if we had records from Genghis Khan, we might find the same thing.

The operative principle is illustrated copiously throughout history: Policy conforms to expressed ideals only if it also conforms to interests. The term "interests" does not refer to the interests of the population, but to the "national interest"—the interests of the concentrations of power that dominate the society.

In their article "Who Influences U.S. Foreign Policy?," published last year (2005) in the *American Political Science Review*, Lawrence Jacob and Benjamin Page find, unsurprisingly, that the major influence is "internationally oriented business corporations," though there is also a secondary effect of "experts," who, they point out, "may themselves be influenced by business." Public opinion, in contrast, has "little or no significant effect on government officials."

One will search in vain for evidence of the superior understanding and abilities of those who have the major influence on policy, apart from protecting their own interests.

The great soul of power extends far beyond states, to every domain of life, from families to international affairs. And throughout, every form of authority and domination bears a severe burden of proof. It is not self-legitimizing. And when it cannot bear the burden, as is commonly the case, it should be dismantled. That has been the guiding theme of the anarchist movements from their modern origins, adopting many of the principles of classical liberalism.

One of the healthiest recent developments in Europe, I think, along with the federal arrangements and increased fluidity that the European Union has brought, is the devolution of state power, with revival of traditional cultures and languages and a degree of regional autonomy. These developments lead some to envision a future Europe of the regions, with state authority decentralized.

To strike a proper balance between citizenship and common purpose on the one hand, and communal autonomy and cultural variety on the other, is no simple matter, and questions of democratic control of institutions extend to other spheres of life as well. Such questions should be high on the agenda of people who do not worship at the shrine of the great soul of power, people who seek to save the world from the destructive forces that now literally threaten survival and who believe that a more civilized society can be envisioned and even brought into existence.

NOTES

This column is adapted from my Edward Said Memorial Lecture at the American University of Beirut in May 2006. The full text appears in *Inside Lebanon: Journey to a Shattered Land with Noam and Carol Chomsky* (2007).

The Somalia Syndrome

"This poor country keeps taking one blow after another," Peter Goossens observed two months ago in an interview with the *New York Times*' Jeffrey Gettleman. "Ultimately, it will break." The country is Somalia, and Goossens directs the World Food Program, which is now feeding some 1.2 million people there—15 percent of the population.

This tragic and tortured land is "marching right up to the edge of a crisis," Goossens said. "Any additional little thing, any little flood or drought, will push them over."

Somalia, war- and famine-torn, is beset from within and without. With a vigilance especially stepped up since 9/11, the United States has reformulated its long-standing efforts to control the Horn of Africa (Djibouti, Ethiopia, Eritrea and Somalia) as a front line in the "war on terror," and Somalia is at its very tip. The crisis in Somalia may be regarded partly as collateral damage from that "war on terror" and the geopolitical concerns reframed in these terms.

As Somalia sinks deeper into chaos, members of the African Union have sent small peacekeeping forces there, and pledged to send more if funding is made available. But they are unlikely to do so, "because there is no peace to keep [in Somalia] in the first place," Richard Cornwell, of the Institute for Security Studies in South Africa, told Scott Baldauf and Alexis Okeowo of the *Christian Science Monitor* in May.

By November, the United Nations noted that Somalia had "higher malnutrition rates, more current bloodshed and fewer aid workers than Darfur," Gettleman reported. Indeed, Ahmedou Ould-Abdallah, the top U.N. official for Somalia, described its plight as "the worst on the continent."

The United Nations, however, lacks the capacity to reach the people who are hungry, exposed, sick and dying in Somalia, according to Eric Laroche, head of U.N. humanitarian operations there.

"If this were happening in Darfur, there would be a big fuss," Laroche said. "But Somalia has been a forgotten emergency for years."

One distinction, hard to miss, is that the tragedy of Darfur can be blamed on someone else, in fact an official enemy— the government of Sudan and its Arab militias —while responsibility for the current disaster in Somalia, like others there that preceded it, lies substantially in U.S. hands.

In 1992, after the overthrow of the Somali dictatorship by clan-based militias and the ensuing famine, the United States sent thousands of soldiers on a dubious "rescue mission" to assist with humanitarian operations. But in October 1993, during the "Battle of Mogadishu," two Black Hawk helicopters were shot down by Somali militiamen, leaving 18 U.S. Army Rangers dead, along with perhaps 1,000 Somalis.

U.S. forces were immediately withdrawn in a manner that continued the murderous ratio. "In the final stages of the troops' retreat, every bullet fired against them was answered, it seemed, by 100," Los Angeles Times correspondent John Balzar reported. As for the Somali casualties, Marine Lieutenant General Anthony Zinni, who commanded the operation, informed the press that "I'm not counting bodies . . . I'm not interested."

CIA officials privately conceded that during the U.S.

operations in Somalia, in which 34 U.S. soldiers were lost, Somali casualties — militiamen and civilians — may have been 7,000 to 10,000, Charles William Maynes reported in *Foreign Policy*.

The "rescue mission," which may have killed about as many Somalis as it saved, left the country in the hands of brutal warlords.

"After that, the United States — and much of the rest of the world — basically turned its back on Somalia," Gettleman reports. "But in the summer of 2006, the world started paying attention again after a grass-roots Islamist movement emerged from the clan chaos and seized control of much of the country," leaving only an enclave adjoining Ethiopia in the hands of the Western-recognized Transitional Federal Government (TFG).

During their brief tenure, the Islamists "didn't cause us any problems," Laroche reports. Ould-Abdallah called the six months of their rule Somalia's "golden era," the only period of peace in Somalia for years. Other U.N. officials concur, observing that "the country was in better shape during the brief reign of Somalia's Islamist movement last year" than it has been since Ethiopia invaded in December 2006 to impose the rule of the TFG.

The Ethiopian invasion, with U.S. backing and direct participation, took place immediately after the U.N. Security Council, at U.S. initiative, passed Resolution 1725 for Somalia, which called upon all states "to refrain from action that could provoke or perpetuate violence and violations of human rights, contribute to unnecessary tension and mistrust, endanger the ceasefire and political process, or further damage the humanitarian situation."

The invasion by Somalia's historical enemy, Christian Ethiopia, soon elicited a bitter resistance, leading to the present crisis.

The official reason for U.S. participation in Ethiopia's over-throw of the Islamist regime is the "war on terror"—which itself has engendered terror, quite apart from its own atroci-ties. Furthermore, the roots of the Islamic fundamentalist regime trace back to earlier stages of the "war on terror."

Immediately after 9/11, the United States spearheaded an in-ternational effort to close down Al-Barakaat— a Dubai-based Somali remittance network that also runs major businesses in Somalia — on the grounds that it was financing terror. This move was hailed by government and media as one of the great successes of the "war on terror." In contrast, Washington's withdrawal of its charges as without merit a year later aroused little interest.

The greatest impact of the closing of Al-Barakaat was in Somalia. According to the United Nations, in 2001 the enterprise was responsible for about half the $500 million remittances to Somalia, "more than it earns from any other economic sector and 10 times the amount of foreign aid [Somalia] receives."

Al-Barakaat also played a major role in the economy, Ibrahim Warde observes in *The Price of Fear*, his devastating study of Bush's "financial war on terror." The frivolous attack on a very fragile society "may have played a role in the rise ... of Islamic fundamentalists," Warde concludes—another famil-iar consequence of the "war on terror."

The renewed torture of Somalia falls within the context of U.S. efforts to gain firm control over the Horn of Africa, where the United States is launching a new Africa command and extending naval operations in crucial shipping lanes, part of the broader campaign to ensure its domination of the world's pri-mary energy resources in the Gulf region and in Africa as well.

Just after World War II, when State Department planners were assigning each part of the world its "function" within the overall system of U.S. domination, Africa was considered unimportant. George Kennan, head of the State Department's Policy Planning Staff, advised that Africa should be handed over to Europe to "exploit" for its reconstruction. No longer. The resources of Africa are too valuable to be left to others, particularly with China extending its commercial reach.

If poor Somalia collapses in starvation and misery, that is merely a sideshow of grand geopolitical designs, and of little moment.

Gaza and the Future of a Palestinian–Israeli Peace

JULY 16, 2007

The death of a nation is a rare and somber event. But the vision of a unified, independent Palestine threatens to be another casualty of a Hamas–Fatah civil war, stoked by Israel and its enabling ally, the United States.

Last month's chaos may mark the beginning of the end of the Palestinian Authority. That might not be an altogether unfortunate development for Palestinians, given U.S.–Israeli programs of rendering it nothing more than a quisling regime to oversee these allies' utter rejection of an independent state.

The events in Gaza took place in a developing context. In January 2006, Palestinians voted in a carefully monitored election, pronounced to be free and fair by international observers, despite U.S.–Israeli efforts to swing the election toward their favorite, Palestinian Authority President Mahmoud Abbas and his Fatah party. But Hamas won a surprising victory.

The punishment of Palestinians for the crime of voting the wrong way was severe. With U.S. backing, Israel stepped up its violence in Gaza, withheld funds it was legally obligated to transmit to the Palestinian Authority, tightened its siege and even cut off the flow of water to the arid Gaza Strip.

The United States and Israel made sure that Hamas would not have a chance to govern. They rejected Hamas's call for a long-term cease-fire to allow for negotiations on a two-state settlement, along the lines of an international consensus that Israel and the United States have opposed, in virtual isolation, for more than 30 years, with rare and temporary departures.

Meanwhile Israel stepped up its programs of annexation, dismemberment and imprisonment of the shrinking Palestinian cantons in the West Bank, always with U.S. backing despite occasional minor complaints, accompanied by the wink of an eye and munificent funding.

Powers-that-be have a standard operating procedure for overthrowing an unwanted government: Arm the military to prepare for a coup. Israel and its U.S. ally helped arm and train Fatah to win by force what it lost at the ballot box. The United States also encouraged Abbas to amass power in his own hands, appropriate behavior in the eyes of Bush administration advocates of presidential dictatorship.

The strategy backfired. Despite the military aid, Fatah forces in Gaza were defeated last month in a vicious conflict, which many close observers described as a preemptive strike targeting primarily the security forces of the brutal Fatah strongman, Mohammed Dahlan. Israel and the United States quickly moved to turn the outcome to their benefit. They now have a pretext for tightening the stranglehold on the people of Gaza.

"To persist with such an approach under present circumstances is indeed genocidal, and risks destroying an entire Palestinian community that is an integral part of an ethnic whole," writes international law scholar Richard Falk.

This worst-case scenario may unfold unless Hamas meets the three conditions imposed by the "international community"—a technical term referring to the U.S. government and whoever goes along with it. For Palestinians to be permitted to peek out of the walls of their Gaza dungeon, Hamas must recognize Israel, renounce violence and accept past agreements, in particular, the Road Map of the Quartet (the United States, Russia, the European Union and the United Nations).

The hypocrisy is stunning. Obviously, the United States and Israel do not recognize Palestine or renounce violence. Nor do they accept past agreements. While Israel formally accepted the Road Map, it attached 14 reservations that eviscerate it. To take just the first, Israel demanded that for the process to commence and continue, the Palestinians must ensure full quiet, education for peace, cessation of incitement, dismantling of Hamas and other organizations, and other conditions; and even if they were to satisfy this virtually impossible demand, the Israeli cabinet proclaimed that "the Roadmap will not state that Israel must cease violence and incitement against the Palestinians."

Israel's rejection of the Road Map, with U.S. support, is unacceptable to the Western self-image, so it has been suppressed. The facts finally broke into the mainstream with Jimmy Carter's book, *Palestine: Peace not Apartheid*, which elicited a torrent of abuse and desperate efforts to discredit it.

While now in a position to crush Gaza, Israel can also proceed, with U.S. backing, to implement its plans in the West Bank, expecting to have the tacit cooperation of Fatah leaders who will be rewarded for their capitulation. Among other steps, Israel began to release the funds— estimated at $600 million—that it had illegally frozen in reaction to the January 2006 election.

Ex-prime minister Tony Blair is now to ride to the rescue. To Lebanese political analyst Rami Khouri, "appointing Tony Blair as special envoy for Arab–Israeli peace is something like appointing the Emperor Nero to be the chief fireman of Rome." Blair is the Quartet's envoy only in name. The Bush administration made it clear at once that he is Washington's envoy, with a very limited mandate. Secretary of State Rice and President

Bush retain unilateral control over the important issues, while Blair is permitted to deal only with problems of institution-building.

As for the short-term future, the best case would be a two-state settlement, per the international consensus. That is still by no means impossible. It is supported by virtually the entire world, including the majority of the U.S. population. It has come rather close, once, during the last month of Bill Clinton's presidency — the sole meaningful U.S. departure from extreme rejectionism during the past 30 years. In January 2001, the United States lent its support to the negotiations in Taba, Egypt, that nearly achieved such a settlement before they were called off by Israeli Prime Minister Ehud Barak.

In their final press conference, the Taba negotiators expressed hope that if they had been permitted to continue their joint work, a settlement could have been reached. The years since have seen many horrors, but the possibility remains. As for the most likely scenario, it looks unpleasantly close to the worst case, but human affairs are not predictable: Too much depends on will and choice.

Containing Iran, "All Options Are on the Table"

AUGUST 20, 2007

In Washington a remarkable and ominous campaign is under way to "contain Iran," which turns out to mean "containing Iranian influence," in a confrontation that *Washington Post* correspondent Robin Wright calls "Cold War II."

The sequel bears close scrutiny as it unfolds under the direction of former Kremlinologists Condoleezza Rice and Robert M. Gates, according to Wright. Stalin had imposed an Iron Curtain to bar Western influence; Bush–Rice–Gates are imposing a Green Curtain to bar Iranian influence.

Washington's concerns are understandable. In Iraq, Iranian support is welcomed by much of the majority Shiite population. In Afghanistan, President Karzai describes Iran as "a helper and a solution." In Palestine, Iranian-backed Hamas won a free election, eliciting savage punishment of the Palestinian population by the United States and Israel for voting "the wrong way." In Lebanon, most Lebanese see Iranian-backed Hezbollah "as a legitimate force defending their country from Israel," Wright reports.

And the Bush administration, without irony, charges that Iran is "meddling" in Iraq, otherwise presumably free from foreign interference. The ensuing debate is partly technical. Do the serial numbers on the Improvised Explosive Devices really trace back to Iran? If so, does the leadership of Iran know about the IEDs, or only the Iranian Revolutionary Guards? Settling the debate, the White House plans to brand the Revolutionary Guards as a "specially designated global terrorist" force, an unprecedented action against a national military branch, authorizing Washington to undertake a wide range of punitive actions.

The saber-rattling rhetoric about "containing Iran" has escalated to the point where both political parties and practically the whole U.S. press corps accept it as legitimate and, in fact, honorable that, to quote the leading presidential candidates, "all options are on the table,"—possibly even nuclear weapons. "All options on the table" means that Washington is threatening war.

The U.N. Charter outlaws "the threat or use of force." The United States, which has chosen to become an outlaw state, disregards international laws and norms. We're allowed to threaten anybody we want— and to attack anybody we want.

Cold War II also entails an arms race. The United States is proposing a $20 billion arms sale to Saudi Arabia and other Gulf states, while increasing annual military aid to Israel by 30 percent, to $30 billion over 10 years. Egypt is down for a $14 billion, 10-year deal. The aim is to counter "what everyone in the region believes is a flexing of muscles by a more aggressive Iran," says an unnamed senior U.S. government official. Iran's "aggression" consists in its being welcomed within the region, and allegedly supporting resistance to U.S. forces in neighboring Iraq.

Unquestionably, Iran's government is reprehensible. The prospect that Iran might develop nuclear weapons is deeply troubling. Though Iran has every right to develop nuclear energy, no one—including the majority of Iranians—wants it to have nuclear weapons. That would add to the much more serious dangers presented by its near neighbors Pakistan, India and Israel, all nuclear-armed with the blessing of the United States.

Iran resists U.S. or Israeli domination of the Middle East but scarcely poses a military threat. Any potential threat to Israel might be overcome if the United States would accept the view of the great majority of its own citizens and of Iranians and permit the Middle East, including Iran and Israel, and U.S. forces deployed there, to become a nuclear-weapons-free zone. One may also remember that U.N. Security Council Resolution 687, of 1991, to which Washington appeals when convenient, calls for "establishing in the Middle East a zone free from weapons of mass destruction and all missiles for their delivery."

Washington's feverish new Cold War "containment" policy has spread even to Europe. The United States wants to install a "missile defense system" in the Czech Republic and Poland that is being marketed to Europe as a shield against Iranian missiles. Even if Iran had nuclear weapons and long-range missiles, the chances of its using them to attack Europe are perhaps on a par with the chances of Europe's being hit by an asteroid. In any case, if Iran were to indicate the slightest intention of aiming a missile at Europe or Israel, the country would be vaporized.

Of course Vladimir Putin is deeply upset by the shield proposal. We can imagine how the United States would respond if a Russian anti-missile system were erected in Canada. The Russians have every reason to regard an anti-missile system as part of a first-strike weapon against them. As is well known, such a system could never impede a first strike, but it could conceivably impede a retaliatory strike. On all sides, "missile defense" is therefore understood to be a first-strike weapon, eliminating a deterrent to attack. Even more obviously, the only military function of such a system with regard to Iran, the declared aim, would be to bar an Iranian deterrent to U.S. or Israeli aggression.

The shield, then, ratchets the threat of war—in the Middle East and elsewhere—a few notches higher, with incalculable consequences, and the potential for a terminal nuclear war. The immediate fear is that, by accident or design, Washington's war planners or their Israeli surrogate might decide to escalate their Cold War II into a hot one.

There are many non-military measures to "contain" Iran, including a de-escalation of rhetoric and hysteria all around, and agreeing to negotiations in earnest for the first time— if indeed all options are on the table.

Hypocrisies and Hope in Annapolis

NOVEMBER 8, 2007

The crimes against Palestinians in the Occupied Territories and elsewhere, particularly since the Palestinians voted "the wrong way" in the Hamas victory last year, are so shocking that the only emotionally valid reaction is rage and a call for extreme actions. But that does not help the victims, and is likely to harm them. Our actions have to be adapted to real-world circumstances, difficult as it may be to stay calm in the face of shameful crimes, in which we in the United States are directly and crucially implicated.

We are approaching President Bush's Annapolis conference on Israel–Palestine, the administration's first potentially serious diplomatic initiative in that conflict.

Ideally, the Annapolis negotiations should begin at the point that had been reached in Taba, Egypt, in January 2001. That week was the one moment in 30 years when the United States and Israel abandoned the rejectionist stance that they have maintained in virtual isolation until the present. And Taba came heartbreakingly close to a possible two-state settlement, with a reasonable land-swap. The conventional fabrication is that at Taba the Palestinians rejected Israel's generous offer. In fact, the conference was terminated abruptly by Israeli Prime Minister Ehud Barak, at a moment when negotiators reported that they were close to agreement.

Perhaps Taba nearly succeeded because the United States

was not there as a mediator. Washington's policy toward Israel–Palestine has long been contorted. "Every [U.S.] administration since 1967, when Israel won a war and occupied the West Bank and the Gaza Strip, has privately favored returning almost all of that territory to the Palestinians for the purposes of creating a separate Palestinian state," Leslie Gelb, the respected policy analyst, observed two months ago in the *New York Times Book Review*. Note the word "privately." Why not publicly?

Gelb cannot have meant that the difference in stance came from fear of the terrifying Israel lobby, since he is at pains to deny the thesis that it is a powerful and intimidating force. So why only "privately"? Perhaps because such an interpretation supports the comforting self-image of the United States as an "honest broker," thwarted in its noble efforts by violent and irrational foreigners, with Palestinians assigned the leading role in the drama.

We know what administrations have said publicly. They have rejected anything remotely of the sort, ever since 1976, when the United States vetoed a Security Council resolution calling for a two-state settlement on the international border (the Green Line), incorporating all the relevant wording of U.N. Resolution 242, of November 1967.

By now virtually the entire world agrees on the two-state international consensus, along the lines almost agreed upon at Taba. That includes all the Arab states, who call for full normalization of relations with Israel. It includes Iran, who accepts the Arab League position. It includes Hamas, whose leaders have repeatedly and publicly called for a two-state settlement, even in the U.S. press. It includes even Hamas's most militant figure, Khaled Meshal, in exile in Syria.

Israel has consistently rejected the international consensus, and the United States backs that rejection fully. Bush II has gone to new extremes in rejectionism, declaring that the illegal West Bank settlements must remain part of Israel. But the Party Line remains undisturbed: Bush, Condoleezza Rice and the rest are yearning to realize Bush's "vision" of a Palestinian state, persisting in the noble endeavor of the longtime "honest broker."

Rejectionism goes far beyond words. More significant are actions on the ground: settlement programs, the annexation wall, closures, checkpoints and much worse. The story continues as the Annapolis conference approaches. Just one example: Israel has just confiscated more Arab land to build a bypass road for Palestinians in order to "push the Palestinian traffic between Bethlehem and Ramallah deep into the desert and effectively bar [Palestinians] from the central part of the West Bank," part of the E-1 development project, east of Jerusalem, designed to incorporate the town of Ma'aleh Adumim within Israel and, in effect, to bisect the West Bank, according to the Israeli peace organization Gush Shalom. "With such policies enacted by the government, the famous Annapolis Conference is emptied of all meaning, long before it convenes."

No realistic proposal has been advanced that does not take a two-state settlement at least as a starting point, along the general lines of Taba. Informal negotiations followed, leading to several detailed proposals, notably the Geneva Accord of December 2002, applauded by most of the world but dismissed by the "boss-man called partner," as Israeli political analyst Amir Oren describes the U.S.–Israel relationship. Without U.S. support, Israel cannot achieve its expansionist aims, which lays the responsibility on us here in the United States.

Plenty of pitfalls are ahead. Some of Ehud Olmert's closest advisers have endorsed a version of the "land swap" policy of the ultra-right Yisrael Beiteinu leader, Avigdor Lieberman. Such a swap would give the Palestinians technical authority over the heavily Arab "triangle" region in Israel, bordering the Green Line. In exchange, Israel would annex the West Bank settlements that encompass precious water resources and valuable land, leaving the rest cantonized and imprisoned, with the Israeli takeover of the Jordan Valley. The inhabitants, of course, are not to be consulted.

In the coming weeks, and the longer term, there is plenty of educational and organizing work to be done, among an American population that is largely receptive, though deluged with propaganda and deceit. It will not be easy. It never is. But much harder tasks have been accomplished with dedicated and persistent effort.

"Good News" from Iraq, Afghanistan and Pakistan

JANUARY 22, 2008

The U.S. occupying army in Iraq (euphemistically called the Multi-National Force-Iraq) carries out extensive studies of popular attitudes. Its December 2007 report of a study of focus groups was uncharacteristically upbeat.

The report concluded that the survey "provides very strong evidence" to refute the common view that "national reconciliation is neither anticipated nor possible." On the contrary, the survey found that a sense of "optimistic possibility permeated all focus groups . . . and far more commonalities than differences are found among these seemingly diverse groups of Iraqis."

This discovery of "shared beliefs" among Iraqis throughout the country is "good news, according to a military analysis of the results," Karen deYoung reports in the *Washington Post*.

The "shared beliefs" were identified in the report. To quote DeYoung, "Iraqis of all sectarian and ethnic groups believe that the U.S. military invasion is the primary root of the violent differences among them, and see the departure of 'occupying forces' as the key to national reconciliation."

So, according to Iraqis, there is hope of national reconciliation if the invaders, responsible for the internal violence, withdraw and leave Iraq to Iraqis.

The report did not mention other good news: Iraqis appear

to accept the highest values of Americans, as established at the Nuremberg Tribunal— specifically, that aggression— "invasion by its armed forces" by one state "of the territory of another state" —is "the supreme international crime differing only from other war crimes in that it contains within itself the accumulated evil of the whole." The chief U.S. prosecutor at Nuremberg, Supreme Court Justice Robert Jackson, forcefully insisted that the Tribunal would be mere farce if we do not apply its principles to ourselves.

Unlike Iraqis, the United States—indeed the West generally— rejects the lofty values professed at Nuremberg, an interesting indication of the substance of the famous "clash of civilizations."

More good news was reported by General David Petraeus and Ambassador to Iraq, Ryan Crocker during the extravaganza staged on September 11, 2007. Only a cynic might imagine that the timing was intended to insinuate the Bush–Cheney claims of links between Saddam Hussein and Osama bin Laden, so that by committing the "supreme international crime" they were defending the world against terror— which increased sevenfold as a result of the invasion, according to an analysis last year by terrorism specialists Peter Bergen and Paul Cruickshank.

Petraeus and Crocker provided figures to show that the Iraqi government was greatly accelerating spending on reconstruction, reaching a quarter of the funding set aside for that purpose. Good news indeed, until it was investigated by the Government Accountability Office, which found that the actual figure was one-sixth what Petraeus and Crocker reported, a 50 percent decline from the preceding year.

More good news is the decline in sectarian violence, attributable in part to the success of the murderous ethnic cleansing that Iraqis blame on the invasion; there are fewer targets for sectarian killing. But it is also attributable to Washington's decision to support the tribal groups that had organized to drive out Iraqi al-Qaeda, and to an increase in U.S. troops.

It is possible that Petraeus's strategy may approach the success of the Russians in Chechnya, where fighting is now "limited and sporadic, and Grozny is in the midst of a building boom" after having been reduced to rubble by the Russian attack, C.J. Chivers reports in the *New York Times* last September.

Perhaps someday Baghdad and Falluja too will enjoy "electricity restored in many neighborhoods, new businesses opening and the city's main streets repaved," as in booming Grozny. Possible, but dubious, considering the likely consequence of creating warlord armies that may be the seeds of even greater sectarian violence, adding to the "accumulated evil" of the aggression.

Iraqis are not alone in believing that national reconciliation is possible. A Canadian-run poll found that Afghans are hopeful about the future and favor the presence of Canadian and other foreign troops— the "good news" that made the headlines.

The small print suggests some qualifications. Only 20 percent "think the Taliban will prevail once foreign troops leave." Three-quarters support negotiations between the U.S.-backed Karzai government and the Taliban, and over half favor a coalition government. The great majority therefore strongly disagree with the U.S.–Canadian stance, and believe that peace is possible with a turn toward peaceful means. Though the question was not asked in the poll, it seems a reasonable surmise that the foreign presence is favored for aid and reconstruction.

There are, of course, numerous questions about polls in countries under foreign military occupation, particularly in places like southern Afghanistan. But the results of the Iraq and Afghan studies conform to earlier ones, and should not be dismissed.

Recent polls in Pakistan also provide "good news" for Washington. Fully 5 percent favor allowing U.S. or other foreign troops to enter Pakistan "to pursue or capture al-Qaida fighters." Nine percent favor allowing U.S. forces "to pursue and capture Taliban insurgents who have crossed over from Afghanistan."

Almost half favor allowing Pakistani troops to do so. And only a little more than 80 percent regard the U.S. military presence in Asia and Afghanistan as a threat to Pakistan, while an overwhelming majority believe that the United States is trying to harm the Islamic world.

The good news is that these results are a considerable improvement over October 2001, when a *Newsweek* poll found that "Eighty-three percent of Pakistanis surveyed say they side with the Taliban, with a mere 3 percent expressing support for the United States," and over 80 percent described Osama bin Laden as a guerrilla and 6 percent as a terrorist.

Amid the outpouring of good news from across the region, there is now much earnest debate among political candidates, government officials and commentators concerning the options available to the U.S. in Iraq. One voice is consistently missing: that of Iraqis. Their "shared beliefs" are well known, as in the past. But they cannot be permitted to choose their own path any more than young children can. Only the conquerors have that right.

Perhaps here too there are some lessons about the "clash of civilizations."

The Unspeakable War

FEBRUARY 28, 2008

Iraq remains a significant concern for the U.S. population, but that is a matter of little moment in a modern democracy.

Not long ago, it was taken for granted that the Iraq war would be the central issue in the presidential campaign, as it was in the midterm election of 2006. But it has virtually disappeared, eliciting some puzzlement. There should be none.

The *Wall Street Journal* came close to the point in a front-page article on Super Tuesday, the day of many primaries: "Issues Recede in '08 Contest As Voters Focus on Character." To put it more accurately, issues recede as candidates, party managers and their public relations agencies focus on character. As usual. And for sound reasons. Apart from the irrelevance of the population, they can be dangerous.

Progressive democratic theory holds that the population— "ignorant and meddlesome outsiders"— should be "spectators," not "participants" in action, as Walter Lippmann wrote.

The participants in action are surely aware that on a host of major issues, both political parties are well to the right of the general population, and that public opinion is quite consistent over time, a matter reviewed in the useful study, *The Foreign Policy Disconnect* by Benjamin Page and Marshall Bouton. It is important, then, for the attention of the people to be diverted elsewhere.

The real work of the world is the domain of an enlightened

leadership. The common understanding is revealed more in practice than in words, though some do articulate it: President Woodrow Wilson, for example, held that an elite of gentlemen with "elevated ideals" must be empowered to preserve "stability and righteousness," essentially the perspective of the Founding Fathers. In more recent years the gentlemen are transmuted into the "technocratic elite" and "action intellectuals" of Camelot, "Straussian" neocons of Bush II or other configurations.

For the vanguard who uphold the elevated ideals and are charged with managing the society and the world, the reasons for Iraq's drift off the radar screen should not be obscure. They were cogently explained by the distinguished historian Arthur M. Schlesinger, articulating the position of the doves 40 years ago when the U.S. invasion of South Vietnam was in its fourth year and Washington was preparing to add another 100,000 troops to the 175,000 already tearing South Vietnam to shreds.

By then the invasion launched by President Kennedy was facing difficulties and imposing difficult costs on the United States, so Schlesinger and other Kennedy liberals were reluctantly beginning to shift from hawks to doves.

In 1966 Schlesinger wrote that of course "we all pray" that the hawks are right in thinking that the surge of the day will be able to "suppress the resistance," and if it does, "we may all be saluting the wisdom and statesmanship of the American government" in winning victory while leaving "the tragic country gutted and devastated by bombs, burned by napalm, turned into a wasteland by chemical defoliation, a land of ruin and wreck," with its "political and institutional fabric" pulverized. But escalation probably won't succeed, and will prove to be too costly for ourselves, so perhaps strategy should be rethought.

As the costs to ourselves began to mount severely, it soon

turned out that everyone had always been a strong opponent of the war (in deep silence).

Elite reasoning, and the accompanying attitudes, carry over with little change to commentary on the U.S. invasion of Iraq today. And although criticism of the Iraq war is far greater and far-reaching than in the case of Vietnam at any comparable stage, nevertheless the principles that Schlesinger articulated remain in force in media and commentary.

It is of some interest that Schlesinger himself took a very different position on the Iraq invasion, virtually alone in his circles. When the bombs began to fall on Baghdad, he wrote that Bush's policies are "alarmingly similar to the policy that imperial Japan employed at Pearl Harbor, on a date which, as an earlier American president said it would, lives in infamy. Franklin D. Roosevelt was right, but today it is we Americans who live in infamy."

That Iraq is "a land of ruin and wreck" is not in question. Recently the British polling agency Oxford Research Business updated its estimate of extra deaths resulting from the war to 1.03 million—excluding Karbala and Anbar provinces, two of the worst-hit regions. Whether that estimate is correct, or much overstated as some claim, there is no doubt that the toll is horrendous. Several million people are internally displaced. Thanks to the generosity of Jordan and Syria, the millions of refugees fleeing the wreckage of Iraq, including most of the professional classes, have not been simply wiped out.

But that welcome is fading, for one reason because Jordan and Syria receive no meaningful support from the perpetrators of the crimes in Washington and London; the idea that they might admit these victims, beyond a trickle, is too outlandish to consider.

Sectarian warfare has devastated Iraq. Baghdad and other

areas have been subjected to brutal ethnic cleansing and left in the hands of warlords and militias, the primary thrust of the current counterinsurgency strategy developed by General Petraeus, who won his fame by pacifying Mosul, now the scene of some of the most extreme violence.

One of the most dedicated and informed journalists to have been immersed in the shocking tragedy, Nir Rosen, recently published an epitaph, "The Death of Iraq," in *Current History*.

"Iraq has been killed, never to rise again," Rosen writes. "The American occupation has been more disastrous than that of the Mongols, who sacked Baghdad in the 13th century"—a common perception of Iraqis as well. "Only fools talk of 'solutions' now. There is no solution. The only hope is that perhaps the damage can be contained."

Catastrophe notwithstanding, Iraq remains a marginal issue in the presidential campaign. That is natural, given the spectrum of hawk–dove elite opinion. The liberal doves adhere to their traditional reasoning and attitudes, praying that the hawks will be right and that the United States will win a victory in the land of ruin and wreck, establishing "stability," a code word for subordination to Washington's will. By and large hawks are encouraged, and doves silenced, by the upbeat post-surge reports of reduced casualties.

In December, the Pentagon released "good news" from Iraq, a study of focus groups from all over the country that found that Iraqis have "shared beliefs," so that reconciliation should be possible, contrary to claims of critics of the invasion. The shared beliefs were two. First, the U.S. invasion is the cause of the sectarian violence that has torn Iraq to shreds. Second, the invaders should withdraw and leave Iraq to its people.

A few weeks after the Pentagon report, *New York Times* military-Iraq expert, Michael R. Gordon wrote a reasoned and comprehensive review of the options on Iraq policy facing the candidates for the presidential election. One voice is missing in the debate: Iraqis. Their preference is not rejected. Rather, it is not worthy of mention. And it seems that there is no notice of the fact. That makes sense on the usual tacit assumption of almost all discourse on international affairs: We own the world, so what does it matter what others think? They are "unpeople," to borrow the term used by British diplomatic historian Mark Curtis in his work on Britain's crimes of empire.

Routinely, Americans join Iraqis in unpeople-hood. Their preferences too provide no options.

Index

About the Authors

NOAM CHOMSKY was born in Philadelphia, Pennsylvania, on December 7, 1928. He studied linguistics, mathematics, and philosophy at the University of Pennsylvania. In 1955, he received his Ph.D. from the University of Pennsylvania and began teaching at the Massachusetts Institute of Technology, where he is Institute Professor Emeritus in the Department of Linguistics and Philosophy.

During the years 1951 to 1955, Chomsky was a Junior Fellow of the Harvard University Society of Fellows. While a Junior Fellow he completed his doctoral dissertation entitled, "Transformational Analysis." The major theoretical viewpoints of the dissertation appeared in the monograph *Syntactic Structure*, which was published in 1957 and is widely credited with having revolutionized the field of modern linguistics. This formed part of a more extensive work, *The Logical Structure of Linguistic Theory*, circulated in mimeograph in 1955. Most of a 1956 version was published in 1975.

In 1961, Chomsky was appointed full professor in the Department of Modern Languages and Linguistics (now the Department of Linguistics and Philosophy) at MIT. From 1966 to 1976 he held the Ferrari P. Ward Professorship of Modern Languages and Linguistics. In 1976 he was appointed Institute Professor, a position he held until 2002.

Chomsky is the author of numerous influential political works, including *Failed States* (Metropolitan Books), *Hegemony or Survival: America's Quest for Global Dominance* (Metropolitan Books), *9-11* (Open Media Series/Seven Stories Press), *Manufacturing Consent: The Political Economy of the Mass Media* with Ed Herman (Pantheon), *Necessary Illusions* (South End Press), *Understanding Power* (New Press), and many other titles.

In 1988, Chomsky received the Kyoto Prize in Basic Science, given "to honor those who have contributed significantly to the scientific, cultural, and spiritual development of mankind." The prize noted that "Dr. Chomsky's theoretical system remains an outstanding monument of 20th century science and thought. He can certainly be said to be one of the great academicians and scientists of this century."

Chomsky lives in Lexington, Massachusetts.

PETER HART is the activism director at FAIR, the national media watchdog group. He writes for FAIR's magazine *Extra!*, and is also a co-host and producer of FAIR's syndicated radio show *CounterSpin*. He is the author of *The Oh Really? Factor: Unspinning Fox News Channel's Bill O'Reilly* (Seven Stories Press, 2003).

NOAM CHOMSKY

HEGEMONY OR SURVIVAL

From the world's foremost intellectual activist, an irrefutable analysis of America's pursuit of total domination and the catastrophic consequences that are sure to follow.

The United States is in the process of staking out not just the globe, but the last unarmed spot in our neighbourhood – the skies – as a militarized sphere of influence. Our earth and its skies are, for the Bush administration, the final frontiers of imperial control. In *Hegemony or Survival*, Noam Chomsky explains how we came to this moment, what kind of peril we find ourselves in, and why our rulers are willing to jeopardize the future of our species. With the striking logic that is his trademark, Chomsky dissects America's quest for global supremacy, tracking the US government's aggressive pursuit of policies intended to achieve 'full spectrum dominance' at any cost. Laying out the rules of militarization of space, the ballistic-missile defence program, unilateralism, the Iraqi crisis and the dismantling of international agreements, he argues that, in our era, empire is a recipe for an earthly wasteland.

'Chomsky is one of the most significant challengers of unjust power and delusions; he goes against every assumption about American altruism and humanitarianism' Edward W. Said

'A superb polemicist who combines fluency of language with a formidable intellect' *Observer*

NOAM CHOMSKY

IMPERIAL AMBITIONS

In this essential new collection of interviews, Noam Chomsky explores the world's most pressing questions with his trademark clarity and insight. The result is an illuminating dialogue with one of our leading thinkers – and a startling picture of America's relentless pursuit of power and its catastrophic consequences.

'Our greatest unraveller of accredited lies' *New Statesman*

'One of the radical heroes of our age' *Guardian*

'Arguably the most important intellectual alive' *The New York Times*

NOAM CHOMSKY AND GILBERT ACHCAR

PERILOUS POWER

The volatile Middle East is a region of vast resources, profound passions, frequent crises, and long-standing conflicts, as well as a major source of international tensions and a key site of direct US intervention.

Two of the most astute analysts on this part of the world are Noam Chomsky, the pre-eminent critic of US foreign policy, and Gibert Achcar, a leading specialist on the Middle East who lived in that region for many years. In this book, Chomsky and Achcar bring a keen understanding of the internal dynamics of the Middle East and of the role of the United States.

Timely, erudite and incisive, *Perilous Power* provides the best readable introduction for all who wish to understand the complex issues related to the Middle East from a perspective dedicated to peace and justice.

'Chomsky has an authority granted by brilliance'
David Goodhard, *The Sunday Times*

He just wanted a decent book to read ...

Not too much to ask, is it? It was in 1935 when Allen Lane, Managing Director of Bodley Head Publishers, stood on a platform at Exeter railway station looking for something good to read on his journey back to London. His choice was limited to popular magazines and poor-quality paperbacks – the same choice faced every day by the vast majority of readers, few of whom could afford hardbacks. Lane's disappointment and subsequent anger at the range of books generally available led him to found a company – and change the world.

'We believed in the existence in this country of a vast reading public for intelligent books at a low price, and staked everything on it'
Sir Allen Lane, 1902–1970, founder of Penguin Books

The quality paperback had arrived – and not just in bookshops. Lane was adamant that his Penguins should appear in chain stores and tobacconists, and should cost no more than a packet of cigarettes.

Reading habits (and cigarette prices) have changed since 1935, but Penguin still believes in publishing the best books for everybody to enjoy. We still believe that good design costs no more than bad design, and we still believe that quality books published passionately and responsibly make the world a better place.

So wherever you see the little bird – whether it's on a piece of prize-winning literary fiction or a celebrity autobiography, political tour de force or historical masterpiece, a serial-killer thriller, reference book, world classic or a piece of pure escapism – you can bet that it represents the very best that the genre has to offer.

Whatever you like to read – trust Penguin.